Soul Whispers

A Path of Remembrance

Genevieve Mc Guinness

I dedicate this book to those of us still hurting; a special request by someone I love deeply.

I also dedicate this book to the little girl in me that walked through what no little girl should ever have to.

This book is for those of you searching for meaning in this world, who know we are so much more than we are told, at a time when everything is changing, and we are being called unto our own paths of remembrance.

We are living in and through extraordinary times right now and this book is a gift of hope, a reminder of the one constant in this world no matter what we meet. This constant is the presence of love.

Book Praise

"Genevieve's writing flows smoothly as it deals with, not only up-roaring conflicts, but with the inner conflicts that almost cripple at times and threaten to deprive our joy for life. The author takes our hand in these so often recognised times of isolation, sorrow and moments when we feel we want to give up. Within these pages are her message 'No, do not go there! Rise With Me and Let Us Trust the Unknown - Together'. And that is the difference. It is felt on every page - the author's soul is with us! "Soul Whispers" is a great title for this very human story."

Alethia Sophia (Anaiya Sophia is a Mystic and Author/whisperer of sacred wisdom. Also, a dear soul mentor who has supported my path of remembrance in many ways over the years. https: anaiyasophia.com

"This book gifts us, men and women alike, an insight into the power of the feminine to bring the gifts of transformation into Earthly life. It does not run away from the difficult questions but shows us a path through the storms, fuelled by a compassionate heart." Mary Rose Stewart- Friend & Soul Sister.

"Genevieve has a gift of helping you remember the magic and the divine. The whispers, the stirrings, and the awakenings are there through your every step, if only we know where to look. This book will help you connect with the threads of wisdom that run through us all and hold you through your time of need – whatever our circumstance and whatever our history" Melissa Amos ~ Soul Mentor, www.melissa-amos.com

"This book is life changing. Genevieve's story is deep, thought and soul provoking. It will be familiar to many. It has stirred up deep memories within me, and it offers hope and beautiful soul offerings that soothe and help us to heal. The way Genevieve has intertwined spiritual practices that will enrich our lives make this book an Oracle that you will always have nearby." Susan Stewart ~ Dear friend, Author of Intermitting Fasting – No Diets Involved,

www.intermitentfast.co.uk

"Reading this, I feel I am peeking through the veils into history, herstory. It is a rich tapestry of one woman's story. I feel activated into a soft beautiful light reading this. I feel activated by the imagery, and I have internal smiles throughout. The author moves through a place of pain into empowerment, her return to innocence, through listening to soul whispers, connection, ancestral and angelic guidance with trust and faith. It is honest, warm, inspiring thought and soul provoking." Karen Cassidy – celebrant, mentor, priestess, and soul sister

"Genevieve is an amazing writer, facilitator, and guide for these times. Her words are a balm for those of us following our souls path. She is a gifted channel, earth-grid worker, and high priestess of the heartwomb. This is book takes the reader from an incredibly grounded, embodied life lived in the waking world and rises from there to the heavens. Read it. Dive into the wisdom shared in these pages. Your life will change. Betinna Essert, High Priestess, Womb Wise woman, dear soul sister of the rose.

Editor's Note:

"It stirred my soul in a rising cry of remembrance. It fired me up and brought me closer to myself. It truly is a phenomenal book in so many ways. It is one that speaks to the depths of the soul and is honestly life changing."

Katie Oman ~ Author, Editor, and Mentor, www.katieoman.co.uk

Soul Gratitude

Deepest Gratitude

To Seamus for holding the fort and being a steady loving support to me whilst I drift off into my creative soul flow.

Love and joy to my children for their divine presence, constant gift and call to more joy in my life. Thank you.

To my parents who extend grace my way often in spite of my constant need to dive into what hurts to heal our inner pain stories and turn them into inner love stories.

To my grandparents in spirit and ancestral lineage that have extended much grace and support my way on this path of remembrance.

I also wish to extend a loving embrace to every woman, friend, soul sister, and mentor who have walked any distance with me on this path of remembrance. Together we remember and call home what has been lost to us. I am blessed with too many to name that has inspired me, mentored me, held me, encouraged me, met me where I am and reminded me of what and who I am when I forget. I love you and thank you.

Special gratitude to my editor Katie Oman, I appreciate the accountability and knowing you were there. To the first readers- Melissa Amos, Karen Cassidy, Bettina Essert, Aletheia Sophia (Anaiya Sophia), and Mary Rose Stewart.

Thank you for your honest reflections which made sure this book could be even more of a gift to those choosing to read it, for the book praise and presence in my life. It is deeply felt and known.

Thank you God/dess, to my soul team, The Angels, Christ, Mary Magdalene, Mother Mary, and Hathor constants in my life. My wise sacred spirit counsel, and my sacred 9.

Soul Whispering
Content

Contents

Introduction

A Beginning

When the soul whispers, we feel it stir us awake from within. It is a place no one else has access to. We feel it calling to us, asking us to listen as the soul calls us home.

The courage for this story to be written began to stir within me was from a place deep inside that was growing tired and weary of all the ways we humans harm one another. The ways in which we use "spirituality" to further shame ourselves for not ascending quick enough.

A path of remembrance is about coming home.

Home to our hearts.

Home to more love.

Home to more compassion.

Home to more acceptance.

If your path of remembrance is feeling more like a chore than a calling into more self-love and acceptance, it's possible you have taken a detour. This book and my story are an invitation to move deeper into your own heart so that you may become softer with yourself. We live in a world that is highly traumatised- it hardens us and makes us hard on ourselves.

This book is a softening, an opening, into seeing yourself clearly that you are as ordinary as you are holy, and there is room for both and all.

My teachings are an invite into the unification of all that is divine and human; feeling this is the ultimate inner union that will gift us the most peace here on earth. With the knowledge that the more peace we hold as humans here on the Earth, the more peaceful we become as a humanity. This in turn would serve us all.

In these moments we feel a whispering in our hearts as they open. Forgotten truths arise and a golden thread begins to weave a sacred remembrance through the core of our beings.

In these moments, our soul is opening us, pouring love into us, awakening us to the divine presence of what lives inside us.

The message I long for you to receive as you read these words throughout this book is to know you are all so loved and held through these transitional times that we all find ourselves walking through collectively.

I will invite you continuously to investigate your own soul whispering and the calls of your heart. To allow yourself to respond to life only from that place.

Hand in hand, heart to heart, bloodline to bloodline, we all get to let out a final breath and let it all go.

We are at this time, I believe, rebirthing forgotten mysteries and memories. It is both a confusing and magical holy time.

Illusions are falling to the wayside as increased truths become known. A fire has been lit. Its flames of restoration have begun to dissolve through our mass dream state, awakening one heart at a time.

Let it burn through all that holds us down. Let it burn through all the lies we have been told and sold. Let it burn through your fears, your worries, and vows, bringing you ever closer to that which is you beyond all the illusions that have denied you access to you.

Imagine in this moment that the words that move through these pages are that of a crystalline waterfall that is pouring in from the heavens to cleanse and clear the path ahead. Imagine every word as a nourishing raindrop of aliveness, inviting you to move with life in celebration of all that lives and exists within you. I also ask you to remember I am but one woman with a story to tell and words that are seeking a space for expression.

I am trusting that if you have this book in your hands that your soul called you to these words. But also know it is possible that not all I invite you into through these pages will land into your soul space as a truth for you.

I ask you let that be okay. Instead, I ask that you approach this book with curiosity, and that you let what feels right and true for you land gently into the heart of your being for safe keeping. Know it will linger on and soften any hardened edges from the very real human challenges we meet in this life.

I must confess that this is the third draft of this book. Twice now it has been written, deleted, and let go of, and yet I know in this moment the words that arrive here and now are the ones I was always meant to share with you.

This book is a holy mix of human life and soul remembrance. To experience a sacred dance which invites in the compassionate unification of our divine and human expressions in this lifetime. It is a story of real life, my life, and the ways in which my own path of remembrance was activated and opened so that I could really hear and unify within the whispers of my own soul. Mostly it is a continuous invitation to you the reader to meet yourself with more compassionate acceptance as I reflect upon and bring to life both my human wisdom and souls' gifts for you to receive.

Chapter One
A Spark

I want to share a written piece that captures the essence of what coming home to myself felt like. It captures the pain of my root trauma; alongside the potency of real-to-life initiations I moved through to be able to hold myself safely and rise into the fullness of who I am in this joy we know as life.

Many Hands

Many hands clawed at her flesh. Often and plenty. Often uninvited. Her body letting her down. Her mind awash with confusion and fear. Her voice frozen. Unable to find or speak her no. Each wanting a piece of her. Each taking from her. Blinding her. Silencing her. Numbing her. Choking her. Denying her. Burying her. Mocking her. Very few took the time to see her.

To feel her.

To know her.

To love her.

Her body, mind and spirit ripped apart, ripped open. Visibly shaken, undeniably vulnerable and raw beyond repair.

Or so she thought.

Her mind and some of those around her would tell her she was. Broken. Washed up. Used. Shamed and named. Whore, slut, dirty, crazy, to name a few. Her heart could see she was often demonised for her pain. Shamed for it. Guilted for it. For her open wounds were so very clear to see. Yet ignored for comfort. For to hold and witness her in pain would mean that they too would have to hold and witness themselves in theirs.

Dare we go there? Into the tears. Into the pain. The shame. The dark. Into the madness. The silence. The fears. Dare we go there? Dare we speak out loud the truth of its roots. And see it for all that it was. And all that it did. Dare we go there? To that place our world prefers we ignore. It would rather we stitch up the gaping wound. Dress it up. Make it clean again. Do not look to it. Do not speak to it. Ignore its obvious seeping.

So, she was silenced and would often hear, "Let it go now. It is over. It is time to move on. Enough." Hushed whispers as she walked into the room. Dare she crumble and implode in their presence? What would they do?

Many saw weakness. Many saw crazy. Some still do. Yet the truth is this- Her fragile body, heart and soul were healing. Finding strength again. Reaching into the depths of her being to rekindle and remind herself of what truly lay within. She was moving through some of the blackest waters into the darkest nights. Alone with herself. Often drowning in her own gaping sores. Wildly diving in and through her torn bleeding wounds. So often, day and night.

Terror would overwhelm her. Fear would paralyse her. Crazy would consume her. She learned very quickly what was required of her. What was expected. What was needed to help others feel safe. Putting her own sense of safety into the background. She learned to stay quiet with what was being shown and brought to her. If she dared show how crazy she really was and speak openly of her journey's truths, terror would consume her. She had not found that place of safety within herself. She was trying though. Breaking through those glass shields of illusionary protection. She was fighting daily hard and fast. Against the demons on the inside.

She was dying and being reborn again daily. She was both clueless yet acutely aware, as alone as she felt, that she was being held by some invisible holy force she had yet to meet and fully trust. She was relearning and coming home to love. She was relearning to trust. She was returning all that was lost to her. Rightfully back to her. Where it all belonged.

She was angry. She was afraid. She was fearless. She was searching. She was opening. She was growing. She was surrendering. She was finding magic in life again. She was laughing. She was crying. She was living. She was drowning. She was winning. She was losing. She was rediscovering. Her worth. Her value. Her power. Her purpose. She was ripping herself apart. More than any other ever could. She needed to. She wanted to. She knew freedom lay amongst the shredding of her being. So, she continued. Then she saw on the inside, a bud, an opening, an entry point to something deeper.

What was it? Curiously moving into the unknown. Sometimes desperately so. Sometimes gracefully so. It was small to begin with. Barely watered, needing light, presence, nourishment, and love. So, she began to water this bud. This bud became a rose, a rose so luminous it overwhelmed her. It created deep resistance to accepting the truth of what lay within. She fought hard to deny herself, until she finally breathed out and let it all go.

She began opening, ripening, birthing. She was thorny, wild, and soft all at once. Her sensual fragrance began to playfully explore and dance again with life and living. Her heart, passions, truths, body, relationships, creativity, soul, being, and connection to this world deepened and enlivened every part of her existence.

All that she once thought was forgotten and lost to her returned in love. She began to witness the fullness of all she was here to be. Making no apologies, no more numbing, distractions, avoiding, denying, or resistance. She stood strong and centred and was diving right in. With an awareness that the woman returning to this world would not be the one who entered this journey, yet she would be more of herself than ever before.

She knew many would be confused by her journey, that many would misunderstand it. Some would be curious, even inspired. She also knew with certainty that permission, admiration, or the thoughts of many would not matter to her.

For she was fully embodying, embracing, and knowing with an awareness of all that she is and was and will be. Fully ready and charged with a life force that all she could ever do now was rise."

That first spark that began the fire in my belly started to rise when I was 15 years old after a freak accident. It was a moment that left me in a very vulnerable state with a man who had claimed my childhood growing up. I was across from him, bandaged from my burns, and fuming on the inside. I was scared and knowing I needed to speak up. After a series of traumatic events, it came tumbling out of my mouth what I had held onto tightly my whole life. The years of sexual trauma, abuse, and violence at the hand of an uncle whose job it was to keep me safe and care for me when my parents were not home. Which was often due to the nature of how life was moving for my parents, as they themselves navigated home and work life balances.

When the words moved out from within me, it felt like the world around me became a blur. I suddenly felt very responsible for all the pain in my family. As though I had opened a gaping wound that no one else wanted to know about for reasons that I could not understand then yet do now.

I have come to understand that not everyone wants or needs to dive deep into the wounds of the past to find freedom in their future. I was made differently and, whilst I did not want to live in the past, I needed to make peace with it to have any kind of future. Yes, that meant revisiting what was painful for us as a family, and especially the child within me. I brought these home truths to light when I could feel that this person was going to move on to another family and weed his way into being of help so he could access the innocence of more children.

Even at fifteen, I could feel my holy no. Not on my watch will this happen and felt I had no choice other than to speak the unspeakable. To this day, it was the hurt and heartache it brought to my parents that was the hardest part to witness. There was no question of whether I was telling the truth, for my truth was met with belief and heartache.

I witnessed this wave of nausea, fear and rage spread like wildfire. Suddenly an awareness of what had been sitting here in the room with us all these years make itself known.

I was supported in ways that made sense in very practical ways. It was reported to the police and the man was removed from our family. I had a visit from a child support team and, most importantly, I was very much believed. Yet, the emotional and mental support was not there, and the only reason for this is that those around me simply did not know how to hold it nor me. It took me years into my adult journey to make peace with the knowing that people can only hold us to the capacity they can hold themselves. It is often rarely personal when we are left holding something hard on our own. It simply comes down to the capacity of what others can hold with and for us as we navigate challenging times.

Years passed in-between that decisive moment to speak my truth out into the world and all that followed. Police, court cases, not so great counsellors, drugs, sex, and alcohol addictions, unsafe spaces and places that recreated much of my original traumas in life. This embedded more of the shame that I would later learn was never mine to carry.

Years of repeating patterns of self-loathing and destruction led to an unplanned pregnancy that would become my guiding light home to myself; one I needed more than I knew. When I fell pregnant, I had no idea who the father was. I had slept with different partners in proximity and the terror of that knowing being known filled my body with fear, judgement, and self-loathing ridicule. I also struggled with the knowing it would be hurting people, people I cared about. I did not even know I was pregnant initially as I was so disconnected from my own body and sense of self. When it finally landed into my awareness, it was through a dream, and I woke up terrified. Upon returning home from a trip away, I let this news sink in, wondering how I would ever be a mother given how I could barely look after myself. I was 20 years old, not making particularly good decisions, and not in a committed relationship.

There were immature decisions made around that time out of fear and an inability to own my recklessness and actions. I simply did not have the skillset within me to take accountability for my actions, and I was not even fully aware of the impact I was having on others; not until I was much older. The one thing I knew in my heart was that I was keeping my baby and I would be a mother.

It never came into my heart or mind once to abort my daughter, who will be twenty-two this year. I knew with the whole of my being that she was a lifeline to another way of living. I stopped drinking and taking drugs straight away.

I faced the shame of not knowing who her father was more than once and it was hard, not just on me, but those I impacted with my deceit and actions based on fear. I managed to move through my pregnancy. Although I was extremely sick throughout, something inside of me was shifting.

Not having the escapism through sex, drugs or alcohol meant I had a clear head for the first time since my early teens. I prayed for the first time in years, novenas throughout to Mother Mary. A novena is a prayer of dedication to a particular saint with a petition to help a certain cause said over a set number of days. I have never known one not to work. Mother Mary was who I was praying to and is still my guiding light. My prayer to her was mostly to be a good mother. I was making promises whilst my daughter grew in my womb to do the best I could to hold her safe and be a mother she would be proud of.

I was having one of those days filled with doubt and unease around my ability to be a mother and be a safe space for my child, when I stumbled across a sign on our main street of the local town I grew up on. It offered readings and, having had an interest in this, I decided I would go in. I still did not know who the father was and was hoping she would give me insight. I walked into the room upstairs expecting to be across a table and have cards drawn. Instead, she popped me up onto a therapy couch and began to place her hands over my body at various points whilst music played.

In my life, at this time, I was emotionally and mentally unregulated, constantly hyper-vigilant, and always alert for something bad to happen to me. I lay there wondering what she was doing, unable to get out of my head, only to find myself suddenly relaxing into what she was doing. I now know it was my first experience of energy work. Afterwards, she shared information regarding my confusion yet gave me no clear answers only the reassurance that all would turn out and that I would be a good mother. I left that room a little spaced out and not grounded. I walked into another little shop- a local charity shop- for the angels above the sign caught my eye. As I walked in, a woman in this space came to me saying, "The angels have asked me to give you this."

With that, she placed a smooth worry stone into the palm of my hands and asked that I hold it daily as often as I could.

She told me I could pour all my worries into this stone. I held that stone daily like my life depended on it, because it did and so did my child in my womb. Something shifted in me throughout that pregnancy, and it felt like I got a brain transplant; everything inside of me was moving differently, I became more and more aware that I had something to live for, to love. When my daughter arrived, a love so big flooded my whole system, a love I didn't know existed and didn't feel deserving of.

I kept looking at this little baby in my arms telling anyone who would hear me how beautiful she was, and here is the thing, she still is, this child of mine. Even though she arrived at my world at a time when my life resembled a trainwreck. Her birth, no matter how she was conceived, course-corrected my life path and led the way for her little brother, who arrived at my womb shortly after. I always felt God in His infinite wisdom knew I needed sobriety for longer than one pregnancy to be sure I would show up in my motherhood more fully. I was pregnant with my son 6 weeks later and this pregnancy kept me home and focused on what was important, which was mothering.

I made a promise to that little girl in my arms in the dark while we were all alone. She was so small, so perfect, so beautiful, so innocent; I was overflowing with love for her. I promised her I would stay. Even though I wanted to leave. I promised her I would try and find a way through to be a happier woman, to be someone she could look to for strength, wisdom, and courage, and to try and find in me all the things I lacked in those moments. I promised to find the innocence of perfection I saw in her and bring it home to me.

By the time my son was born, I knew I had made a grave mistake in living with his father. He was also experiencing the very same realisation and we knew we were not healthy together. Within six weeks of our son's birth, we separated.

I simply now believe that each of us had so much to unpack solo before we could really show up in a relationship mature enough to hold it long term. We tried, we really did try, and it hurt us both when it ended. We struggled as young adults with the aftermath of that hurt for years after and it impacted the one person that was enormously important, which is and always was our son. It is something I imagine we both harbour certain regrets over.

At this time, I found myself in a taxi with the clothes on my back and no money to my name to start my life with myself and two babies under the age of 1. I had no idea where I would start or how I would do it, I just knew it was the right thing to do and I still believe this to be true to this day. I found myself in my parents for a short stay until I found a place for us to live. The place I found was all I could afford, and it was deemed unlivable by the local council. I was working part-time on single parent benefits, starting back at higher education, and trying to piece my life together one heartbeat at a time. These years were difficult. I was often very lonely, I was a chain smoker, lived on my nerves, and even got on my own nerves at times. I was often insecure about my ability to mother and carve out a life that would make them proud. On the surface I looked like I was managing well. I was holding the threads of my existence together the best I could, even if loosely, and so much was falling through the gaps. I look at my older children in awe for I grew up with them. I was often stressed and anxious, and not always making the right decisions. Pivoting my life often and plenty to make it easier for me and for them. I finally got gifted a new home. Thankfully, an old schoolteacher approached me and said she could help.

She worked with a charity called St. Vincent de Paul. The house was a little two bed bungalow and to me it was a lifeline. It was an opportunity to make a home, a real home for me and my children. I was so excited! I was back at art college, money was starting to feel easier, and life was too. Not long after, another house through St. Vincent de Paul came up, which was a three bedroomed with a separate kitchen and living space. It was close to my parents and had both a front and back garden; it felt like winning the lottery. This time was abundant for me, for I moved in and at the same time accessed money I had been given through the court as compensation at age 18.

I never respected this money nor saw it as a gift when it was first received. I felt it dirty with his hands on it- the man who had sexually abused me. It was money I did not spend wisely when I was younger. This time I could choose differently, so I did. I used it to decorate my new home. I bought the furniture I needed, put down new floors, painted the whole house, and even gifted it away. Slowly I felt like my life, even though hard, was beginning to feel better. I was still feeling that pang of loneliness and really wanted a family for me and my children, as in what we are told family is: father, mother, and children.

On reflection, I already had a family- me and my children were it. It was me that didn't feel enough, my children always were enough. My home was always filled with other kids, my garden too. We had daytime discos, late night movies, face painting, garden tents, art and play in-between me working, training, teaching, and going to university.

I remember one night feeling the weight of it all. I was alone in my sitting room; the fire was lit, and the kids were asleep. I was working on a project, and this overwhelming sadness and tears came. I often felt guilt and shame because different fathers conceived my children. I was feeling it all in my little sitting room by the fire and I sent a prayer up to find love that was real, and that was right for me. I felt this warm embrace of a hug; it felt so loving. I knew without knowing how I knew that it was my paternal grandfather in spirit that was with me. I felt his love and a wave of forgiveness wash over me. I heard as clear as anything that everything was going to be OK. I knew and felt both him and my grandmother with me always those days, like a silent guiding light helping me make better choices for me and my children. I rested into that love for what felt like a forever moment, and I went to bed knowing as alone as I felt, I was not. I carried this feeling with me in the weeks that followed.

A few weeks later, a friend who I had known since childhood invited me out to see a band. I was open but it wasn't fully a yes. I went to her home last minute deciding that, yes it would be a clever idea to go. I made little effort in terms of what to wear and threw on denim jeans and a green halter neck top. The band was her brothers' friends in a local bar that was called The Bound for Boston. I arrived ready to go and noticed that her brother Seamus was joining us. I had always been attracted to Seamus and I knew that something was going to happen between us always. It had previously when we were both younger- a kiss here and there- but not for years.

To give some background, I recall arriving to his house with my children to meet his family, I grew up a lot in their home, which felt like home from home to me. I remember visiting with my children and my son's father. Seamus was there, and his mom was pouring us tea, delighted to meet the babies again. Seamus was in one chair, while my son's dad was on the other, and I knew in that moment I was with the wrong man. As crazy as its sounds, I always knew I was to travel this life path with Seamus. This is an example of a soul whisper landing into the heart and feeling it as truth.

I felt it at 15 years old and now suddenly here I was, almost 23 with two children, feeling in my heart like my grandfather in spirit brought this whole experience into being so we could begin our lives together. I went to the bar to see the band with a feeling Nicola had set this whole thing up for us. Nicola left us for a moment, and we ended up kissing. He took my number, rang me before I got home and the rest, we say, is history.

Our relationship moved slow and fast all at once. He proposed within the year. However, we did not move in fully together until our daughter Tegan was born in 2006 and we did not marry until 2009. In these years, so much began to stabilise in my life. We were both back at university growing up in ways that mattered.

He grounded me and I opened him up to possibilities. He sees everything very black and white, whilst I joke with him that I am his rainbow. We complimented each other and rose in each other all our wounds to explore and meet. We had so much to learn and were passionately in love with one another. Like most couples in today's world, we had truly little modelling of what a healthy relationship was, so we were learning together and doing the best we could with what emotional tools we had available.

Sometimes this looked and felt secure, at other times it was incredibly hard to trust that we would be okay. On reflection now, it is extremely easy for me to see the ways we were not healthy and in need of support, yet I can also see all the ways we were willing to really try and figure those parts out. The way I met our hard parts was by acknowledging that I wouldn't want to meet it with anyone else. Our most intimate relationships are the most intimate reflection of who we are and what we want or do not want in life. We can work with what is reflected to us, or we can deny the reflections and run from what is hard and ourselves all at once.

We offered something to one another that no one else ever could. Life was shifting and changing dramatically. We both qualified in our chosen career path- him as a structural engineer and me as an art teacher. Finances were stabilising, careers were stabilising, and we had a third child. We had upgraded our home, choosing to leave the house I had rented for years as a single mother and move into our first home together. So, now we were also officially living together. We were planning our wedding, the date had been set, and we were excited about life. Excited about each other.

We fought a lot, kissed, and made up a lot. It was what we did. We also grew up a lot, supported each other's dreams and ambitions. We got healthier in mind, body, and spirit which for me was a genuine indicator of more being right than wrong.

Chapter Two
May you Remember

Then something shifted dramatically in my life. A little girl came into my awareness through my daughter. She shared something about what was happening to her in her home. I listened to my daughter as she shared and the horror of what this little girl was living through came flooding into my awareness. I tried to help her through all the proper channels- social services, garda, and school.

I felt powerlessness. I felt rage. I felt lost and aware that the systems there to support our children simply could not, would not, or did not know how.

This experience threw me back into the trauma of my own childhood, with my own pain and disappointment at not being protected looming large. I could not eat, sleep, or be at peace; something big and deep was stirring within me.

I was on my knees crying after a night of no sleep, angry at GOD. How can this be happening? Why do these things happen? I raged to GOD, I cursed at GOD, said out loud to not bring me anyone I cannot help. That if GOD was going to bring people my way, to help, to make sure I have what I need inside of me to help them. I told Seamus that I could not stay where we were anymore. I asked to move.

We found a house within two weeks. It was the most beautiful house we had ever lived in. The moment I walked in, peace descended into my body. I found a book which opened up a channel in me and I experienced the Archangels, Mother Mary, and our Lord Jesus Christ. I was shown the light of our soul. The truth of who and what we were and are.

From this moment onwards, my life changed, I changed, how I see this world changed, and how I met my life changed. I felt a love this world has no words for. It is something that is felt and met. People would call what happened to me an awakening moment, others would call it a psychosis. I would simply know it was Love's presence making itself known so it would never be forgotten again. This was a homecoming to my soul's energy and presence, a sacred remembrance, one I invite you into with me so that you too may remember.

Angels began to communicate with me regularly. Mother Mary would show me my reflection in the mirror- my soul's energy and my auric energy field. There was so much shared with me at this time. About whom and what we are beyond the human, for example. There was so much to take in, yet what stayed with me the most was that feeling of love, which expanded through my body for weeks on end.

I was blown wide open and became a truly clear channel in a moment.

A channel for and of love

I was channeling daily guidance from the Angelic Realm through my days.

Angel Gabriel would share about the children of the world. Angel Raphael would show me how to work with my energy body to heal old hurts. Angel Michael showed me what peace looked and felt like and how to protect my peace of mind.

In the pages that follow I will share part of what was shared with me in channelled writings I journalled about at that time.

Gabriel's Message about the children

"You will lead, and so many will follow, your hearts are true and unyielding. Go forth, dear child, and no longer be afraid of your power and truest purpose here on earth. So many still need guidance and fear themselves. They will feel safe and feel love from you. Which will chase away their fears and allow them to honour their truest divinity and beauty. You see this beauty in all things and must share what you know and feel. For you came from love and a place of wanting to free the human condition of all that holds them back. Take time to reflect and speak with us often; we will gently lead and pave the way as you have asked and prayed for. Allow help to flow to you. Pay attention to your ideas and thoughts as they are as precious as gold now and will flourish and blossom as radiantly as a spring meadow. Allow the divine to flow through you unto the earth and feel this divine energy embrace all that you are and all you desire for Earth. Fill your mind with joyful thoughts, fill your world with joyful actions, fill the children with blessings of love. Teach them well, so they too can feel and embrace their unique divinity. Do not be afraid if they make choices that frighten you- trust they are right for them and they too are being guided joyfully through the Earthly planes. Embrace your ideas and work with the children, teenagers, and young adults who are vulnerable and anxious of their surroundings. Give them back their power. They are ready to embrace all they came to be. Show them the love you know is real and trust yourself. The world is awaiting on your arrival, so embrace all that you came to be. Love AA

Gabriel."

Raphael's message about healing

"As you begin to open to your multi-dimensional existence, you will see, feel and become witness to false hooks that play out as stories, thoughts, and patterns of behaviour, which are stored within your energetic field. These stories have you believe you are powerless, unable to shift the direction of your life, unable to access source light, energetic wisdom, or codes of remembrance. As these stories of old make themselves known to you, I invite you to call upon my presence and imagine I am there with you, wrapping you up in a healing balm of light. Imagine I am there with you with the softest of ribbons wrapping up your energetic field. I am soothing the aches from false stories and filling you with a lightness that shifts and harmonises your energy field into being more responsive to what is true within you. This will help you access more of your soul's gifts with greater ease and soothe past and present hurts. Love AA Raphael"

Michael's message of peace and protection

"The human mind is a gift and a place of disruption. I am offering my shield of protection and sword of truth. The sword can be used to cut through the deceit of the mind that pulls you into separation from your divine spirit. The shield can be used to protect you from your own thoughts that cause you great harm. Call upon my presence in your times of doubt, when you feel lost, insecure, and uncertain about life and the choices being brought to you. Ask that I cut through to the truth and make it known to you, and that I shield you from anything that would mean you harm. Love AA Michael."

This moment with the Angels redefined everything about who I was and the direction my life would take from this moment onwards. For you to understand this shift, I will walk you through the varied soul pathways home I took to discovering more of myself than I ever knew possible.

It is my belief as I write these words for you that there are many paths home to the love that exists within us.

This love exists within you because you are love. You do not have to do anything to be with this love; it is what you are.

Imagine for a moment the vastness of creation. God and Goddess. The multitude of ways creation can play with creation upon this joy we know as life. Then look at the billions of ways we get to explore that here on this one planet for the betterment of ourselves and one another.

This sentence moved through me one day as I reflected on this part of our human expression that seeks to be right.

"Go judge your friends chosen path and declare that they are wrong in your righteousness. For, in that moment, you judge all of creation and misunderstand the gift of exploration offered to us on this planet."

I ask one thing as you continue to journey with me through these words that will weave together a journey that to some may seem fantastical and unbelievable, to others a sacred nod of recognition. This is a knowing that you are not alone in your experience- for some, it will be the first invitation into something beyond anything you have ever known in this life.

The one thing I ask is that you keep this in heart and mind that I am as ordinary as the day is long and as extraordinary as the mystery that has unfolded in this life I lead. As are you. As extraordinary as what I share with you is, what has arrived at my being as the number one truth is that our humanness in this sacred mundane existence is the most divine part of it all.

To capture the depth and essence of what lives in the invitation of each word spoken, I felt to share a written piece where I felt the mother of everyone speak through me.

Chapter Three
The Invitation

She called and I answered

The Invitation

"I am the Earth herself and I am the heavens above

I am an embodiment of what lies beneath you. I am the vastness of what rises above you. I am all that you are and all that you see in me. I am a portal of endless possibilities, if you dare to seek through me.

I am the fullness of what breathes through you, gifting life moment after moment, long after you have stopped breathing me in, and forgotten my presence.

I am there.

With you still.

Breathing.

Filling you up.

With life.

I am what catches your breath in those moments of sheer wonder and lust as you gaze upon my body, and the endless luscious landscapes that sustain and feed you daily.

I am the dirt beneath your feet that grounds you and protects you so that you may be reminded of your humanness, your strength, and the path that you are here to walk.

I am the mother of all mothers. So much is born from me and through me unto you

I am the light that sustains you through your darkest hours. That teases you into the madness of your mind. In the hope that your frantic grasps at life in this space will create a fight like no other for freedom against these manmade cages of lifeless wanderings

I am the fertile seed of creation that burns through your passionate hearts in the hope that you will hear my call and answer it with the depth of passion I feel for you. I am the ecstasy you seek through your exploration of what it is to be sacred as you find your way home to me.

I am the silence in-between each in breath and out breath as your soul takes a moment to invite you gently inwards to gaze deeper into what is truly being revealed to you in your moments of doubt.

I am all that is sacred. I hold all that is true and holy in deep reverence for safe keeping, only gifting it to you when you know and see the truth of what lies within. I am the pleasure felt within the body when love's touch opens the flow of connection like no other. I am the rage of pain that swells deep within your womb when you have ignored me for too long.

I am the roar of enough when I see you take from my daughters and sons what was never to be taken. I am the changing winds that cast you into the wilderness to find what you have forgotten when you came through your mother's womb of love into the world. I am the wisdom of your soul that begs you to be still long enough so that you may learn to be with me a moment longer than your busy lives allow.

And each new moment begins to stretch you beyond all that you have ever known. I am the re-birth. I am the reemergence. I am the re-igniting. I am the re-alignment. I am the re-remembering of who you are.

I see you as the phoenix that rises from the ashes of destruction to find that you and I are the same holy love of creation. Yet we are also wholly different, for you carry a unique vibrational frequency that only you can and only you ever could.

And it is this that the world needs now. It is you that I am calling home. It is you that I am calling into action. It is you that I am calling into hope. It is you that I am calling into faith like never before so that we can together rise into the fullness of love that knows no bounds or limits. Where the fierce love of holy creation can bring balance to what has been shamelessly skewed for personal gratification.

It is you created from the womb of the mother and the heart of the father that is feeling these words as your own.

Can you hear me now?

Do you feel me now?

Will you answer my call?

I felt and answered this call daily. At first it wasn't SHE I was hearing, instead I was answering the whispering of my soul's longing to connect me to the most divine part of myself and it all began with the Angels.

It is possible some of you reading this are unfamiliar with Angels, so for this reason I will share what I have come to understand what an Angel is, so you know moving forwards what and whom I am referring too.

My understanding of what an Angel is, is this. An Angel is a multidimensional being of light here to support us on this life path should we choose to ask for their assistance. They do not belong to one religious faith and are guardians of universal law, Gaia, and the many souls who incarnate upon this planet.

Angels are available for all divine humans on this path. I believe they can assist us with finding our personal power as they help us clarify and take a stand for our lives and what we believe in. They encourage us to honour our truth, to let go of what doesn't serve us, reassess our relationship to ourselves, our lives, each other, and the Earth.

At a time in my life when I had lost faith, Angels invited me back into a life of hope, of sacred remembrance and into a path of sacred daily devotion that ignited a realisation that I had the power in me to redirect my life path, as well as opening up to more love.

Archangel Michael became what I can only describe as a bodyguard within my mind. I invited him to shield me from any thoughts that would mean me harm, and this is exactly what he did. I was not a person who could easily tap into gratitude with ease. My first go to thoughts due to my trauma were always of fear, pain, and the very worst-case scenario. In the beginning, I leaned heavily into affirmative inner talk. I had a little black book that I filled with prayers, channelled messages, symbols, and affirmations.

This little book went everywhere with me, I would read it morning and night. I felt very guided to work in this way and it helped me massively reframe how I thought of myself and my life. I still have this little black book of hope that I can hold onto in my hand and its pages are battered and old.

It holds within it my dreams from that time. There are so many ways to work with our Angelic Allies in this life. I choose to keep it simple and prayer-like, likely due to my Catholic upbringing. However, I am a lover of prayer and feel deeply connected to that which is unseen through spoken word.

At this time in my life, the Angels brought me to many ways to collaborating with them. I could feel them energetically in the room with me. Each would feel different so I could familiarise myself with who was who. Archangel Michael was a cool breeze at my feet, Archangel Raphael was a warmth in my heart, Archangel Gabriel was a tingling sensation upon my crown.

They each felt and spoke differently and carried a different vibration. Archangel Michael felt extraordinarily strong in his presence. I would even say father like- a very loving fair father like energy that would redirect my thoughts and actions towards more integrity. For example, he would help me to redirect my energy and focus if I started to spiral into patterns of behaviour that were destructive for me.

Archangel Raphael felt very soothing and gentle. I often describe Archangel Raphael like a soothing balm of love, and a soft warm blanket that wrapped you up in a way that you just melted into it. Raphael's voice felt softer too. His energy was always encouraging you to clean up your act, for example, to choose something nourishing for the body, to drink less alcohol, and to rest more. I always feel more energised when working with Raphael. I found his energy very soothing for my heart and guidance enormously powerful for my mothering and marriage.

With Gabriel I felt like I opened to a world of wisdom not previously known to me. I would receive continuous downloads of information (which I now know as channelling) about children and teens. Information on what would be moving through our world and the ways in which these children would need held and supported.

Examples and reasons to call upon a certain Angel

Raphael ~ For health and wellbeing

Michael ~ For protection

Gabriel ~ Clear communication

Ariel ~ Life purpose

Sarah ~ Empowerment

Faith ~ To release stress

Daniel ~ To help with grief

Celestina ~ For self-expression

Cassiel ~ To heal heartache

7 ways for you to connect with the Angels

- Ask them directly to make themselves known to you.
- Place your hand upon your heart, close your eyes and meditate upon an Angel of your choice.
- Write a letter to your Angel of choice with your special request.
- Ask each Angel for a personal calling card. This is a way for you to identify with the changing vibration of each Angel.
- Create a sacred space of connection and prayer.
- Light a candle in devotion to your Angel of choice.
- Ask for a sign from your Angels that you will instantly recognise when it arrives.

The more I opened to the Angel's presence in my life, the more I felt like my awakening was more to do with my children and the children I now also have in life. There was one moment when I was meditating with the Angels. I was directed to get up and go into the room where my three children at the time were playing together on the floor. I could see with my physical eyes their auric fields around them. I saw their higher soul energy slightly up from their bodies, which looked like translucent colours; I find it hard to describe in words. I was half-startled and half in awe just looking at them. I saw how at peace their soul selves were and was invited into making peace with the part of me that often felt at war on the inside.

This was the part of me that never felt quite good enough or worthy of these incredible children to raise as my own. I always carried a guilt around the fact that my children had different fathers. As though it made us less of a family somehow in comparison to others, at least in my mind. I carried a level of shame around how my family was made, not knowing, or understanding that this was creating an energy dynamic within my home that fed a story of not being worthy or enough.

When I became aware of this, I started to shift and make decisions around changing that inner story. For this story implied I was ashamed of my children, but I was not. I was ashamed of past versions of myself that at that point in time I had little to no compassion for. It was in this moment that genuine real healing started to occur for me around my shadow energy. It would be years later that I would begin to understand the gift and significance of being able to meet myself time and again in the underbelly of my existence.

The Angels explained to me how our children choose us, the parents, how we are all interlinked. They shared with me how on a soul level our children know us in our entirety and know our strengths and perceived short comings. I say perceived as often what we humans see as shortcomings are part of the soul medicine we are here to bring.

The Angels taught me so much in that first year of working with them in 2009. They taught me how to meditate, how to breathe properly, how to stay in my body and feel what was arising, and they taught me how to listen to my heart and higher counsel.

They showed me our inner chakra energy centres and how to work with that energy and bring it into my body through symbols, prayer, focused attention, and colour to heal my emotional centre, past traumas and limiting belief systems that were holding me back from believing in myself.

Soul Gift – A brief introduction to the Chakra energy system.

What is a chakra?

Chakras are an energy vortex that exist within and outside of the physical body. They are a felt and seen as a wheel of colour that are constantly moving within the body. Each chakra within the body is linked to our major organs and nerve bundles within the body. Many know of the 7 main chakra energy centres that are known as the seven centres of spiritual power within our bodies. There are others located outside of the body. I am going to share about 9 chakra energy centres briefly to gift you a feel for how working with these energy centres can support your physical, emotional, mental, and spiritual experience.

Where are chakras located?

There are seven chakras located along the spine, starting at the tip of our tailbone and moving up through the body to the top of our head. The energy of our chakra system extends from above and below our bodies, to the front of our bodies, and up the back of our bodies. The other two chakra vortexes I will share about that are located above our head and below our feet.

Why is it important to connect with, work with and clear our chakra energy system?

Benefits of working with your Chakra energy centres.

- Regulates our emotions
- Supports our mental health
- Helps us reach and stay in the energy of peace.
- Supports us in accessing better health and wellbeing.
- Connects us with our personal and collective soul purpose
- Guides us to knowing wisdom beyond this world by helping us access higher levels of consciousness.
- Supports us in finding greater balance in our lives.

- Guides us in the opening of kundalini (shakti – our life force)
- Deepens our relationship to the Earth
- Helps us access information to understand our karmic blueprint – life lessons and blessings
- Helps us access ancestral wisdom so that we may use this wisdom to guide our current life path.
- Opens our soul gifts to express them with ease. □ Opens our hearts to give and receive more love
- Connect to our intuition and expand our sensory gifts in this life.

There are so many reasons why working with our energy centres in this way can support us in this life. I am hopeful this brief overview gifts you some understanding of its importance.

I am now going to briefly share a little about each of the 9 Chakras so that you may have a starting point of reference if this knowledge is new to you. For those of you who are aware of this wisdom, this is a little soul reminder of each Chakra's colour, name, location, purpose, and soul gift.

Soul Star Chakra

Soul Star ~ 8th Chakra ~ Sutara

Known as:

The Seat of the Soul

The universal heart

The holy star

Colour

Gold and white

Location

It is located three to four feet above the crown (head)

Purpose

Holds our soul's wisdom, mission, purpose and connection to source. A link to our Akashic Records – (a soul library of our every incarnation)

Soul Gifts

Clarity

Connection

Ease

A SOUL STAR MEDITATION

- Close your eyes.
- Feel the sensation of your in breath and out breath.
- Open your heart.
- Call upon Christ light.
- Raise your hands upwards.
- Open your hands, palms facing upwards.
- Imagine connecting with the golden light of your soul star.
- Call in any wisdom that wishes to become known.
- Bring your hands down place them onto your heart.
- Journal on what you received.

Crown Chakra

Crown Chakra ~ 7th Chakra ~ Sahasara

Known as:

A supporter of our higher consciousness, wisdom, and emotional wellbeing.

Colour

Violet/Purple

Location

Top of head and is linked to our pituitary gland, pineal gland and the hypothalamus.

Purpose

To connect us to our personal passions, visions, and purpose.

Soul gifts

Regulation

Hormonal balance

Memory support

Access to past, present, and future timelines

CROWN CHAKRA MEDITATION

- Close your eyes
- Feel the sensation of your in breath and out breath
- Open your heart
- Call upon the presence of Angel Jophiel
- Imagine your crown opening up like a purple rose beginning to bloom
- Imagine Jophiel placing within your crown a diamond
- Feel this diamond open and gift you soul wisdom to help you on your path
- Sit for as long as you need to
- Journal on what you discover

Third eye Chakra

Third Eye ~ 6th Chakra ~ Anja

Known as:

The inner eye

The mystical eye

The brow chakra

Colour

Royal Night blue

Location

Centre of the forehead, between our brows. Linked to the clitoris
(female) penis (male)

Purpose

Inner sight, advanced intuition, connection to spirit

Soul gifts

Trust ~ Knowledge ~ Peace within

To bring us into a higher state of consciousness

THIRD EYE MEDITATION

- Close your eyes
- Feel the sensation of your in breath and out breath
- Open your heart
- Call upon the energy of Angel Raphael
- Focus your attention/imagination on the third eye
- Imagine it opening
- Feel Raphael pour a healing balm of light into your third eye
- Ask for clear inner sight
- Journal on your experience

Throat Chakra

Throat ~ 5th Chakra ~ Visuddha

Known as:

The Purifier

Colour

Blue

Location

Pit of the throat – linked to both our cervix and throat.

Purpose

To help us express ourselves with confidence and speak our truths. A sacred gateway that allows energy to move into the upper chakras.

Soul gifts

Trust ~ Truth ~ Confidence ~ Authentic expression

To help us move beyond shame into our highest expression.

THROAT MEDITATION

- Close your eyes
- Feel the sensation of your in breath and out breath
- Open your heart
- Call upon the presence of Angel Michael
- Ask Michael to gift guidance on where your heart is blocked.
- Ask to clear these blocks.
- Feel the energy clear
- Journal on your experience.

Heart Chakra

Heart Chakra ~ 4th Chakra ~ Anahata

Known as:

A gate opener to more love

Colour

Green and pink

Location

Centre of our chest. It is known to support our heart, lungs, chest, thymus glands, arms, and legs.

Purpose

To unify the lower and upper chakras, our holy human and sacred divinity.

Soul gifts

Better emotional wellbeing

Compassion

Acceptance

Love

HEART MEDITATION

- Close your eyes
- Feel the sensation of your in breath and out breath
- Open your heart
- Call upon the presence of Angel Ariel
- Ask for support for your soul's mission
- Feel anything weighing heavily on your heart lift up, clearing the path ahead
- Allow yourself to feel the expansion of that clearing
- Bathe in the expansion
- Journal on your experience

Solar Plexus ~ 3rd Chakra ~ Manipura

Known as:

The city of jewels

Our power centre

Our inner sun

Colour

Yellow

Location

Belly – Below the navel. Connected to our digestive system, liver, stomach, pancreas, and bowel.

Purpose

To support our internal and external power, will, strength, and stamina.

Soul gifts

Regulation of our nervous system

Fire (energy) into all our organs, systems and processes in

life.

SOLAR PLEXUS MEDITATION

- Close your eyes
- Feel the sensation of your in breath and out breath
- Open your heart
- Call upon Angel Uriel
- Feel your energy drop into your belly
- Imagine a golden sun
- Feel it brighten
- Feel its power
- Expand this light and power throughout your body
- Journal on your experience

Sacral Chakra

Sacral Chakra ~ 2nd Chakra ~ Svadhisthana

Known as:

The navel chakra

The dwelling place

Colour

Orange

Location

Womb(feminine)/Hara(masculine). Sexual organs. It is located at the front of the body, at the level of the pubic bone.

Purpose

To support the awakening of kundalini life force (shakti), sacred sexuality, our creative life force.

Soul gifts

Connection ~ Creativity ~ Vitality ~ Passion

SACRAL MEDITATION

- Close your eyes
- Feel the sensation of your in breath and out breath
- Open your heart
- Call upon the presence of Angel Gabriel. Rest your hands upon your womb(feminine)/hara (masculine).
- Feel the energy of Gabriel activate this energy centre
- Ask for a soul message
- Receive this message
- Journal on your experience

Root Chakra

Root Chakra ~ 1st Chakra ~ Muladhara

Known as:

Base chakra ~ The foundation

Colour

Red

Location

Resides in the perineum: Male (inside the perineum, between the scrotum and anus). Female (On the posterior side of the cervix)

Linked to our spine, joints (knees and legs), tendons, ligaments, muscular and skeletal systems. It supports our adrenals. Purpose

Stablises our foundations ~ Supports the physical body. Is the seat of our Kundalini

Soul gifts

Patience ~ Security ~ Trust ~ Wellness ~ Support

ROOT CHAKRA MEDITATION

- Close your eyes
- Feel the sensation of your in breath and out breath
- Open your heart
- Call upon Angel Gabriel
- Hand over any worries you have about your earthly life
- Ask for guidance on a particular worry in your life
- Feel a message of reassurance come to you
- Journal on your experience

Earth Star Chakra

Earth Star Chakra ~ Vasundhara

Known as:

The sub personal chakra

Our grounding point

Daughter of the Earth

Colour

Of the Earth

Location

Below our feet, around 12 -18 feet below our physical bodies.

Purpose

Connection to Gaia (Earth)

Connection to our soul and earthly ancestry

To ground our chakra system, purpose, and life force to our collective purpose

Soul gifts

Guidance ~ Grounding ~ Connection ~ Purpose

EARTH STAR MEDITATION

- Close your eyes
- Open your heart
- Feel the sensation of your in breath and out breath
- Call upon the presence of Angel Sandalphon
- Imagine you are drawing all of your energy down into the Earth
- Imagine feeling fully supported by the Earth
- Imagine how strong this makes you feel
- Call all this energy upwards. Let it rest with in your heart
- Journal on your experience

This time with the Angels learning all that I was, was also a time I was cocooned in what felt like a lasting peace that no one could penetrate or disrupt, and it seemed to last for such a long time.

This elated sense of knowing that we are never alone, that we are always loved, that we are always seen, that we are a miracle in a human body experiencing a planetary experience of polarity in a dance between forgetfulness and remembrance all at once. Show me a room full of grief and right there within it is a room full of love right alongside each other. Show me a room full of doubt and there will be a teacher of unapologetic confidence. Show me a room full of pain and right there will be someone there able to hold it safely.

They would spend hours with me, guiding me back to my heart and to art. In this year alone there were so many experiences that have been forever imprinted into my being forever. They are a continuous reminder of what and who I am as I move through this life, often still awkward and clueless. For the more I learn, the less I seem to know.

This time in 2009 felt like I moved into a university of wisdom that just kept on giving. More and more I would receive and fill up. I would hear the Angels singing. This sound has never left me, the closest I have ever heard it Earth side from a divine human was as recent as 2019. Her name is Mei-Ian. The first time I heard the Angels sing forever changed me, I wanted to go home to be within that energy every day of my life. I recall being woke up one evening and meditating downstairs with the Angels. Within my inner vision I saw this diamond blue light tunnel rising upwards and I was being lifted through this tunnel of light. Circled around me was legions of Angels clapping and welcoming me home. I know how this may sound to some, yet I know in my heart that I was at home within the presence of Angels. I also knew I was here with a purpose, which was to guide others home to the love that lives in them. For when you feel that love, you too will be forever changed yet more of yourself than you ever imagined possible.

Chapter Four
Art is a Healer

I was training to be an art teacher at the time, which I loved. However, I had stopped creating my own work. I recall one evening being woke up by Raphael and making my way downstairs. I hadn't done any personal art for a long time, but there were always art materials, and I was guided to some chalks. I lifted the chalks and began to work on a large piece of paper I had on the floor. On my knees I was scribbling away. It wasn't making much sense to me, but I didn't feel like I was the one guiding my hand on the page. It felt very trance-like. I was brought to my feet and encouraged to shift the paper upside-down and to my amazement I saw very clearly steps and a large Angel. I wrote underneath it 'manifest your dreams'.

This painting was created on the floor of my living room with chalks and became a constant inspiration to believe in and follow my dreams. From I was a little girl I had dreamed of being an artist and a writer. I never knew what I would create or write about, I only knew I was here with those gifts within me, and I wanted a way to express them.

I am sharing this chalk drawing with you in the hope you feel this energy and message and that you too remember what was placed inside of you to bring to life on this planet at this time. I often feel if we could think back to when we were children and what we loved to do as a child that this is the best way for us to reconnect with the truest soul whispers within that we are here to express. We are closest to the innocence of our expression as children and sadly as we grow, due to many external factors, we lose sight of our soul sparks and often find ourselves searching for it as adults.

Until this moment I hadn't really considered that I had any power over what my life could look like. I didn't know what manifesting was, I had to look it up. It turned out there was loads of teachings and teachers on ways to manifest your dreams and that the Angels were inviting me to trust in God and them to begin re-creating a life path that felt more fulfilling for me and not the train wreck it had so often been until that point.

Truth be known, I still jump a ride on the occasional train wreck, only I seem to be able to catch myself quicker these days and shift direction with more ease. Thank GOD I say.

Speaking of manifesting dreams, that little black book I shared about it was called "Little Book of Wisdom". It was filled with prayer and intentions, love and light with each word and action. I was all about the love and light for a period in my life and, you know what, I needed it. Lord knew I had lived enough darkness for a time. The lightness was needed and welcomed, and I drank it in until the moment came when I could no longer hang about there and pretend the hard stuff wasn't still wreaking havoc on the inside. For now, though, let's chat about some of the sparkly parts of manifestation which came to pass in 2016, after a gut wrenching few years in the underworld of my own existence, which was to have a solo art exhibition.

This exhibition became a celebration of the Angels and the energy they bring into our lives. It was called "Heavenly Angels" and honestly was something I felt deeply proud of. As someone who had created art since a child, this felt like a celebration of my soul's gifts. These paintings moved through me over a period of three weeks. I had the exhibition planned and the paintings weren't moving through. It was a huge lesson in trust, in my gifts, and in my connection to that which is divine within me to show up in the creation process. I had been channelling paintings for years now. Each painting was a shamanic initiation, and each painting brought home soul parts- a version of myself that got lost in this life. I coined this time before: A Journey in Life Through Art. For that was what it was. To give a little context and history, I had always been an artist, a creative soul. It's the one part that stayed with me and was wholly and completely encouraged throughout my childhood.

I don't ever recall a time that I was not encouraged in art and creative pursuits. It was often my saving grace, that thread of joy in an otherwise often bleak existence at various points in my life. As a child, I was often drawing fae-like creatures, women wearing the earth. It was assumed and encouraged that I was a designer- a fashion designer, I kept that dream alive for many years until I arrived into art college studying textiles and fashion design only to discover I was not a great designer and more of an eccentric artist who was now lacking the freedom to just create for joy's sake.

I continued with the degree though, as a door of opportunity had presented itself with support so I could better my life and create an income beyond government single parent payments to support myself and my two children.

I felt proud I was achieving, yet not exactly lit up about being a designer. I was too messy for starters and lacked a certain discipline designer's naturally have. I did do well and decided teaching made sense as I had already for many years done various volunteering and workshop facilitating, and I enjoyed that environment. I now know I was likely channelling art as a child and my little earthy fae like beings were likely my little soul friends making themselves known. At least knowing what I know now about this wonderous universe, we are all part of.

Back to how I started creating my own art again. As previously shared, it began with the Angel art 'Manifest Your Dreams'. I was reminded of my many bus journeys to and from Belfast to university when a thought used to drop into my mind- it was always the same 'A Journey in Life Through Art'. So, in between that painting, I had married and done a training course on IET- integrated energy therapy. I was feeling good about my life and the decisions being made. I was feeling abundant living in the most beautiful home I had ever lived in. There was fun, lightness, and love, and I felt like I was genuinely landing somewhere solid for the first time in my life.

In this Little Book of Wisdom years earlier before this exhibition, I had sketches of inspiration and written on one of my affirmations about creating and hosting a solo exhibition. So much of what was written in that little book, has come to pass, in so many ways, some in ways I could never have imagined when I was scribbling my heart out on its pages in the beginning.

If you are new to imagining what is possible for you, for your life, this can help.

Soul gift ~ A technique to help with manifestation

Here is a simple effective practice that can help you.

- Purchase a journal
- Fill it with colour, images, words, inspiration, quotes, and sacred prayers or intentions if prayer is not your thing.
- Spend time writing into your dreams and offer daily gratitude's for the life you are dreaming into being.
- Read it daily, nightly, as often as humanly possible.
- Say ~ "Thank you, thank you, thank you."

Use your imagination to gift it feeling, sensation, and detail to create the energetic connection to the dream you are manifesting into your life. Spend time imagining what having this in your life would feel like. Give it detail- the more you can imagine the details, the easier it will be for you to feel it as real and already in your life. Gift yourself feeling, open to the sensations in your body, imagine opening your heart and visualise a golden cord of love expanding outwards towards the desire you are calling into your life.

Soul tip ~ Remember this

"Remember your desires and dreams are divinely placed within you to live fully in this life."

I promise you that little book of imagination, of sacred possibilities, will gift you more than you can ever imagine right now in this moment.

Let this share be an invitation into sacred trust and then open your heart to receive the soul whispers that will nudge you into the life you know you are here to live!

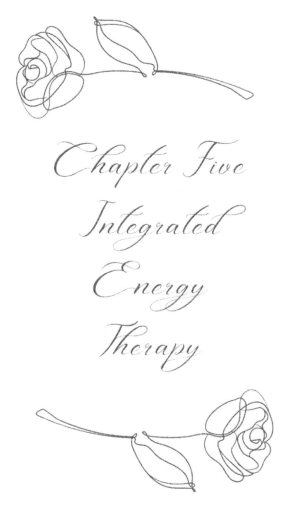

Chapter Five

Integrated

Energy

Therapy

I briefly mentioned IET and felt to expand on what it is. IET is Integrated Energy Therapy, and it is a direct hands-on healing modality channelled by Steven Thayer through Angel Ariel's guidance. It has transformed my life in ways that still ripple through, and I am now a teacher of IET and have taught many students since 2016. I was guided to IET through Angel Raphael where I was led to a woman in Derry who offered this energy therapy. Not long after, I connected with a cousin of mine who was working with IET regularly at that time and Siobhan became one of my biggest supporters on this path home to myself. Her support, presence, wisdom, and love gifted me so much confidence to continue this path I now found myself on.

I was still trying to do the art teaching thing, but then I broke my ankle. For those that do not know, our bodies like to show us energetically what is happening. A broken ankle represents conflict around where we are going and worrying that we can't support ourselves. At this time, I was a mother of three, out of university a year, and doing teacher training. We were in our first year of marriage, and Seamus was working away from home with the intention I would join him after my teacher training. Then my ankle broke, and I broke a little too with it. I was missing him hugely and we decided to make the move as a family a year earlier than intended.

To give context about why this move surprised me the most, I loved where I was living. All my family lived there, and my children were content enough in the schools they were attending. I was living in a beautiful home and all I met in this place was the most miraculous life changing experiences. The sacred soul remembrance, the Angels, my reconnection to God, our wedding celebration. Moving made no sense logically on so many levels.

We were living in a small town known as Buncrana. It is what I believe to be one of the most beautiful parts of the world- Ireland, County Donegal, by the Atlantic Ocean. We made the move there when I was almost 13 years old. Moving to this town is what put a stop to the sexual abuse I had previously been living through. I was born a Derry girl; my mother grew up in the bog side of Derry. The area is steeped in history around the troubles of Northern Ireland, most known for Bloody Sunday, which also happened to be the day my own mother's mother was buried. I wish to honour her for a moment, her story was overshadowed by collective history for a moment in time.

A bloody history where many people suffered greatly in Northern Ireland and for many years after, which was never okay. I felt it's impact even though I was not born in it. Many of us do. Due to the timing of my grandmother's death and burial, it was almost felt like grieving her wasn't allowed because of what happened that day in the lives of so many. Yet it mattered, grieving her mattered, my grandmother mattered- to her children and to her husband, my grandfather; their grief mattered very much. I am opening my heart in this moment to acknowledge what possibly wasn't. As I write right now it feels important that I do, I can almost feel her in the room with me- her and my grandfather.

There was a moment on my journey when my grandfather arrived in spirit offering me a red rose and a white rose and told me to keep moving forwards and that I was to trust my path. It felt strange and comforting connecting with him in spirit like this after his passing. This message came at a time when I was feeling a lot of distance between me and my family of origin due this to new way of living and expressing myself.

As for my grandmother, I am named after her and I am often told I look like her. Our name Genevieve means "connector of women, tribe of women" Which I didn't find out until I was much older. I love knowing the meaning of my name and feel I have grown into its meaning in this life. I did not ever meet her; she is the grandmother I never knew yet used to talk to in my heart as a child with the belief that she and I had a special connection because we carried the same name. She passed away when my own mother was only 13 years old, leaving behind her children and my grandfather. I cannot imagine what that must have felt and been like for my mother and her siblings. For my own mother to move through her adolescence into womanhood and motherhood without her mother there. A crucial time in a young woman's life and growth.

My mother was with me as I birthed my first born into the world and held me supportively as I navigated those first tentative months as a young mother. I imagine she longed for hers often and still does, especially in those times when she birthed us into the world.

We left Northern Ireland when I was almost 13 years old. Left our local council estate to move to what felt like the mountains to a wee Derry girl. I recall my dad joking with us about moving in beside the sheep and about what our walk to school would be. It turned out the laugh was on us, and we moved to the middle of nowhere with, yes, sheep for neighbours and a walk to school that took more than a little adjusting for us all.

Our first day there we all walked through a place known as Swans Park, and I fell in love. I met the bridge and felt instant ease, at home. This bridge is still the one I move towards when I take a shamanic journey to the beat of the drum. Whilst we walked through Swans Park, it really did feel like a wonderful new beginning for us all and it was in lots of ways.

This move was important in many ways to me personally as it was also a goodbye to the man who had harmed me most as a child. Even though Buncrana was only a 20-minute drive from Derry. To many in Derry, including my uncle, it may as well have been Narnia. I could taste the freedom from his holding, the call of the ocean, and sand in my toes, and knew instinctively this little town would always hold a special piece of my heart as it would hold many of my hurts into healing. It still does, even though my teen years were turbulent and somewhat soul destroying. I strengthened in that town- I cried, I wailed, I fell apart, I let go, I let be, and I found some of my closest friendships that are still thriving and alive today. This small town held my maiden years, her wildness and vulnerability, her adventures and pain stories at once.

Soul gift ~ A way for you to honour your maiden/teen years

- Feel into that time and reflect upon all the stories you hold about yourself for that period in your life. Write down all the pivotal life changing moments
- Feel into the strengths and courage it took to navigate those times
- Write down all the significant relationships at that time and your feelings about them
- Feel into the compassion and forgiveness needed to honour this time
- Spend some time writing a letter of gratitude to your inner maiden/teen, thanking this part of you for this time in your life.
- Write down all of things you wish someone had said to you.

In this moment, I wish to honour my maiden and all that she carried by sharing a piece of writing that releases the shame that was never hers to carry. It speaks into self -forgiveness and how to navigate the betrayal of the feminine and reclaiming innocence.

The first time I got called a whore I was 10 years old, she slapped my face and screamed whore at me, wiping the lipstick I was playing with off my face. I knew at that moment she knew what he was doing and that she was carrying his dark shame and secret, just like I was.

I knew also at this moment, even though she was an adult woman, that she was fully blaming me the girl child for his dirty secret. She was protecting him and was angry with me. I had no choice in that at that tender young age. I accepted her blame, I fully accepted that I was the whore even though I had no idea at that moment what a whore was. I accepted that it was me that was dirty, shameful and the cause of his actions. I took on the story of this is my fault- I am the one to blame for this. At that moment, it was the first time I felt completely betrayed by the feminine.

She was his wife, and she knew, she always knew. I had a feeling she knew yet it wasn't confirmed as truth until that moment and when we locked eyes- tears stinging in mine, rage spilling out from hers.

I spent more years angry and afraid at her betrayal and lack of courage to speak up and protect me than I ever did by him and his actions. Which sounds weird, but it is true to how I felt. I met this woman 3 times one year in 2018. For the first time in around 25 years.

The first time I saw her at the Doctors Surgery, I looked at her and she didn't know me. I just sat there catching her eye, willing her to see me and recognise me, but she didn't. She was old, weak and clearly unwell.

The second time I passed her across the bridge, and I made a promise to myself if I saw her a third time I would speak. I had no idea what I would speak to her or if I would see her again.

The third time I walked right into her at a furniture store. We came face to face along a very narrow aisle, so I kept my promise to myself, and I spoke her name and said hello. She looked confused, then I saw the flood of recognition in her eyes, along with a wash of shame, guilt and I would also say fear.

I didn't expect what came out of my mouth after that. We had a very brief conversation. I asked how she was, she did me. She went to speak to my children, and I stood in front of them and said: "God bless", moving forwards to end our conversation. I meant it, for she needed those blessings more than I at that moment. I walked away strong, centred, and fully at ease in myself.

I went about my business and saw her a little while later, crouched over on a bench and visibly upset. A part of me wanted to console her and offer her some reassurance, but the wiser part of me knew that I was not to blame, that it was not my shame, and that the tears she bore were not my fault. I left her with all that she slapped into my being that day with her rage, fear, guilt, shame and the word "whore" and took back what was mine, the truth of my innocence and the goodness that lay within me.

It wasn't until much later in my life that I would learn what the word 'whore' meant and feel the ferocity of its second judgement as I lived out my trauma in my formative teen years.

A few weeks later I was out running in the hometown where I lived my teen years, and I suddenly felt very vulnerable, unsafe, afraid to be seen, and self-conscious. Old mind stories took hold. I felt that old anxiety rise and my face redden as a wash of shame rose through my body.

I knew it was rising to let me know it's time to let it go now, so I ran across the Crana Bridge, the one that shows up when I do shamanic journeying.

I began to see within my inner sight, as I was still running, myself shatter into a million pieces as shards of glass broke away from me. These shards of glass were etched with words like whore, slut, bitch, tramp, and easy- all the words that had etched their way into my consciousness as true. It was a story so wrapped up in shame that warped my perception of myself and the truth of who I am.

These shards of glass, this false exterior of lies that had built its existence in and around me as true, shattered and broke away into a million pieces. I could see myself rising and embodying my truth, my innocence and my courage to be seen as I truly am even more.

I came to the water by a local beach and stopped. Sitting on some rocks, I opened myself up to the Earth and her power. I felt her take me home to a part of myself that was looking to come back to me. To integrate and be at one within me. I went to the ocean and used the waters to bless me, bless my crown, my throat, my heart, my solar plexus, my womb, and my hands and feet.

I got up and carried on with my run towards Fr. Hegarty Rock, where I rested quietly doing some practices that I love to do. These were normally hidden in the dark by candlelight, in the safety of my room and alone, yet there I was in the wide open and out of hiding. I was offering prayers of gratitude for this journey, for this place that held me as I lived out my pain, for the ocean that soothed me through those years, and for this place I have come home to after all these years....

I got up and walked home in this town I love, by the ocean I love, no longer afraid to be really seen as I am...."

I was left Buncrana 7 years before I rooted into something of myself that was important to find. Consciously choosing to leave what had become my home since I was 13 years old was a huge deal for me. I was so close to my family, my sisters, and their children- we would see each other daily. We were far from perfect but show me a family who is. Yet we hold a thread of connection that, no matter where our lives take us, we find our way back to one another one way or the other.

On reflection, I can now see why it was so important for me to leave, so that I could find independence from my family, my past, my pain, the pain I felt responsible for bringing into my family's experience, and so I could find some courage to live out loud who I was fast becoming.

I don't believe this book would have been written had I not moved. The Angels, energy work and IET became one of the biggest catalysts of soul support on my journey home to myself as the years moved on. This is an energy therapy that supports us into releasing the pain of the past and reaching into the joy of the present. It works with us physically, emotionally, mentally, and spiritually. What I personally found most supportive about working with this energy therapy was that I could heal some of my deepest trauma without having to relive the pain each time something cleared. It is a safe non-invasive energy practice that supports us through this life and its many hurts. It supported me hugely through this massive life transition of leaving my home and family so I could stretch into more of who I was here to become.

Here I was in a new country, in a new home, with our eldest three children. Almost three weeks into our move to England, Basingstoke to be exact, and our belongings had not yet arrived. I hated our house, it was small, with a shoe box kitchen, awful décor, and we were sleeping on blowup beds we had to purchase. We were living out of suitcases we had brought with us, waiting on our belongings to arrive. To say it was a bumpy ride from the moment we arrived, would be a bit of an understatement.

On the plus side though, our kids settled very quickly into school life, and I began to immerse myself in life, with meet ups in the community. I found sisters of the heart in England. Sisters from every lifestyle, from every country. Sisters in Christ and sisters of the Moon. Sisters who became like family to me, and I to them. Who supported our family into settling. Who extended kindness and brought opportunities my way on a human and soul level. Soon I really started to enjoy living in England. I enjoyed the freedoms of not being in a small town. It was a fresh start where no one knew who I was before, and people were meeting me as who I was in the present. I never knew how much I needed that freedom in my life until I had it.

I felt at ease with these women, like I had walked this life path with them before. We learnt and grew so much together. Their families became our family. These women treated me like their sister, and I felt safe with these women in my life. I learned a lot about devotion and faith in their company and every one of them, too many to name here, carries a place in my heart where they all reside. As I grew in confidence around this new life, I began to get bolder in my expression online.

I felt a sense of safety to speak more about the Angels. I had sisters of the heart there with me in real life, encouraging me to share what I would share with them in the privacy of our circles. Having this encouragement meant more to me than they ever possibly could have known. I began to share more of the Angel messages being brought to me. I was connecting with increasingly like-hearted and minded souls through this great online sacred web known as social media. I discovered an app called Meet Ups. I saw there was an event locally and they felt and sounded like my kind of people who I could ride along this sacred path of remembrance with. The online world became a world of connection and opened ways for me to connect in real time with people I would not have met otherwise.

I went to events, and, through Archangel Michael's guidance, I felt called to speak and connect with some of the women in there. Within these gatherings I met some wonderful friends who are still constant in my life. I was humbled by the kindness, the welcome, and the ways in which they desired for me to share my gifts. I remember one of them asking me how long I had been a channel. I am going to admit I did not know what a channel was nor that I was one. For those of you now wondering what a channel is- a spiritual channel is someone connected to their psychic gifts who can connect to and bring messages from spirit. Through their intuitive senses, they speak/share the wisdom brought to them. I was doing this with Angels and Spirit Guides with great ease at this point because, for me, it had become normal and not something I thought of as special or grand. To be honest, I still do not. I know everyone is and can be a clear channel, as we are all connected to and born of the same breath of creation.

What are ways to support your energy into being a clear channel

- Meditate
- Receive energy healing

- Pray
- Journal
- Get creative
- Be in nature
- Treat your body with care and love
- Learn about energy
- Connect with your soul guides

How can I improve my ability to be a clear channel?

Work with and develop your intuitive channels some call these the 4 Claires or 4 "C's".

1. Clairaudience ~ Where you hear spirit
2. Clairvoyance ~ Where you see spirit
3. Clairsentient ~ Where you sense and feel spirit
4. Claircognisance ~ Where you know what you know with no explanation to how you know.

4 soul tips to develop these channels.

1. Clairaudience ~ slow down, listen to the world around you, spend time in silence, spend more time listening than talking.
2. Clairvoyance ~ Work with clearing your third eye, clear any feelings of mistrust so you can begin to trust in yourself and the world around you.
3. Clairsentient ~ Spend time in nature, slow down and ask to receive the energy of the room you are in, create, play and explore the sensations alive in this world.
4. Claircognisance ~ Pay attention to your dreams, thoughts and what you say. Journal and ask questions to let your pen guide your words and answers.

I was invited kindly by a woman into her home to hold Angel meditations. I would spend time writing down my meditations that were channeled in the moment, print them off, and read off these pages for the people who were attending to join. I found the more I did these, the less I needed to print anything off. More and more I was asked to trust in my ability to open to my soul gifts to receive the words and share them. This time was a fascinating eye and heart opening time for me.

These circles of support became my learning ground. They proved to be the foundation upon which all of what I bring and do now was built. I was building friendships and sisterhoods, I was using my IET, and my artworks were taking me on a shamanic soul retrieval experience with every paint mark drummed unto the canvas.

I was attending regular shamanic drumming circles. These teachings and experiences have never left me and always called me further home to the beating drum of my own heart visions. My visions were fast and thick. I journaled daily, I meditated daily, and I walked daily. I connected with my spirit team and Angels all of the time. I was sharing more about how these experiences were healing my past and current hurts.

I was dying and being reborn all at once.

This painting "Rebirth" captured the essence of what I was fast becoming yet not fully living. I could feel her in me, in the women around me, in the Goddess as she made her faces known to me through the art of my soul.

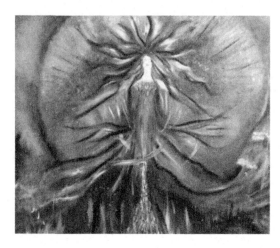

I was becoming more aware of the ways I related in an unhealthy manner in my most intimate relationships; I was seeking, learning, growing, developing and tasting life on a whole new level. At this time, every painting brought with it a message, a gift for me and others to receive. People were finding me through word-of-mouth. I was attending spiritual fairs and meeting genuinely gorgeously interesting people with whom my entire world opened. My ability to quickly discern what and whom was absolutely right and good for me was turning up the volume.

A divine human soul reached out to me. She caught a glimpse of my artwork online. She invited me to her home, into her community, her world, and we quickly felt deep heart resonance and still do. She now lives in America, and we journey in and through similar cycles of joy and hope together still. She is a continuous source of inspiration, not only to me but to all those she touches. She is a multitalented creative life force of vibrancy whose gifts are endless. She had just began building an incredible open forum for Artists who painted Spirit guides, Angels, and our light being friends, as well as the universal beings Pledians, Sirians, and Acturians. I had no idea how wide open my world was about to become.

What is a spirit guide?

From my understanding, a spirit guide is a soul guide who has lived a human life at some point. Someone who understands the trials and tribulations of a human incarnation. That shows up within our energy field as a support to us on our path of remembrance.

What is a universal soul guide?

From my experience, this is an energy, a soul vibration, a guide from another planet. They may or may not have had a human incarnation. They too are available for support as we journey home to more of ourselves in this life.

How do I connect with mine?

My own guides came through my creativity, my paintings, my art, my time writing and in nature. I encourage others into these activities and to also begin a dialogue with their soul/spirit team. Ask the question- "who is here with me to support my journey?" Wait for the answer.

Soul gift

A soul practice to support your journey and connection to that which is unseen.

- Get some paper
- Get some chalks – crayons or paints
- Create some sacred space (a quiet place where you will be undisturbed, light a candle, play some music)
- Close your eyes
- Imagine your heart opening
- Ask to connect with your soul's essence
- Imagine your crown chakra is opening
- Imagine a light move upwards from your crown into the celestial realms

- Imagine you are connecting with one of your soul spirit team
- Feel their energy conncct to yours
- Receive the information through your crown
- Open your eyes
- Begin to lift the colours you are connected to
- Use these colours to create and draw whatever shapes and forms come your way
- Allow yourself to feel the words being felt through the journey of creation
- Journal about your experience

A Soul whisper ~ Remember this

"Deepen this practice through the exploration of symbolism and colour meaning as you will receive more information and understanding about your soul image."

My Journey in Life Through Art was about to take on a whole new meaning. That little God given brown box of oil paints that had been handed to me by my childhood best friend as I left the Emerald Isle of Ireland became the beginning of something new and wonderful; a calling home to that which I was born to do. Which was to paint. The very first painting I did was of a fairy sitting on a little mushroom with light cascading down over her little presence as she was resting into the earth.

There was one painting though that changed how I experienced my art gifts for ever- it was one I agreed to paint for Frankey. That gorgeous soul who invited me to be part of her soul art community. This is still active by the way and details of how you can connect with her will be at the end of this soulful tale of mine.

I would always create sacred space to paint at this point, though it was still in my living room/dining room, with blankets on the floor as the children attended school. I would light candles, offer some prayer, and set the intention for the one I was painting for.

I would call IET energy into my hands, place this energy upon the canvas, and begin to paint. There was never an outline. To this day, my channelled works move through the same way. I bring the first colour or colours up and begin to move them over the canvas. I wear glasses all the time in my ordinary day living since I was 15 years old. When I paint, they come off. I paint with my hands and mostly ditch the brushes. I play shamanic drumming beats or other instrumental that inspires my movement and connection. As I continued with Frankey's artwork, I notice this beautiful blue light being come to life. I heard her speak and I felt her presence and love for Frankey, I let her guide my hands and heart onto the canvas.

I began to doubt what I was painting as I painted her striking white-blonde hair and almost alien-like features. I was being invited into trusting, opening, and surrendering into this experience with full faith this was what wanted to come through for Frankey. Energy Art and spirit paintings are a way to bring through a psychic impression for the one receiving of their loved ones, spirit guides, light codes and Angelic guides. I completed the painting, took a photograph, and shared the message. These paintings are often shared with a personal soul message for the one receiving. I was only just learning to trust in this gift from my soul for others to receive and it was a journey into believing what was coming through. To my surprise, Frankey knew this guide and cried upon seeing her on the canvas. No one had ever brought her through before and they had been journeying together for a long time. Frankey gifted me faith in my gifts in a way no one else did at that time. I loved her then and I love her now. From that moment onwards, my Journey in Life Through Art took on a whole new meaning and service to those who felt called to receive from me in this way. Sometimes in this life all it takes is one person to see you in your fullness for you to really see what has always existed within you.

This beautiful spirit guide for a beautiful divine human in the painting below brought home to me a new faith in my ability to bring through sacred guidance beyond this world into the hearts of those of us here.

As I deepened upon this joy we know as life into the many soul parts that were arriving home, I began to feel more the call of the drum. Each time I journeyed with the drum, I would come home and paint. Its sound took me places I had not known were possible. My body surrendered to the beat, and I leaned into trusting this way of being to access more of my own innate wisdom and threads of existence. I had never heard of shamanism; I had no idea this was a way of loving, living and breathing for humanity. I did not know of its ancient roots upon humanities path, or the gift it would bring my way. It was a gift that kept on giving, opening me further to what lived inside me, activating more and more of my intuitive gifts, and clearing my inner worlds so I became a clearer channel in service to love. Definition of

Shamanism- Is a soul path practiced by indigenous peoples, characterised by the belief in an unseen world of Gods, demons, and ancestral spirits responsive to shamans that travel between worlds to connect with and work on the soul.

An invitation arrived to receive in ceremony with grandmother drum that had been travelling all around the world under the care of its people, with the intention to bring more peace upon our heart's minds, bodies, souls, and the Earth itself. I recall the drive through the countryside of southern England to reach the home of a gorgeous soul I met along my journey home to myself. She opened her home to us to share food, ceremony, soul, song, love and really drop deep. After a sacred pipe ceremony and working with grandmother drum, we all sang each other's names to one another.

Can you imagine the energy and rite of passage that is to have a whole community of people there singing your name to you? It is a moment that has never left me. I felt every sound of my name land into every cell of my body, and it felt like another layer of my soul arrived and anchored more fully in than ever before. Tears of gratitude fell. I felt a deep gnosis within my body that this was something that would feel powerful and soulful once a child entered the world.

I mean can you imagine a newborn? If you are a parent, I invite you in this moment to imagine you are there with your newborn in your arms, filled with love. Imagine you invite all your family into a sacred space to be with your child and welcome them into the world by singing their name. Every word carries its own vibration. Every letter carries its own vibration. Imagine the impact this would have on the child's energy upon its arrival into our world and lives. I was a grown adult and I felt it, and, in that moment, I felt how potent and powerful it is to have your name sung to you. Some would say we choose our own name on a soul level before we arrive. A wise wombyn once shared with me, as I was preparing to birth my sixth child into this world, the importance of a sacred pause when our babies crown at birth.

In this moment we, the mothers, and the child, access all the soul wisdom they need to know including their right name, if we take a breath and moment to access it. Many women pause in this moment of birthing, often feeling they cannot go on.

Taking a breather, we sometimes stop altogether and feel we cannot go on. What if this moment was recognised for what it was- a sacred moment, a pause as our baby's crown and download all their soul's wisdom before coming Earthside.

It is this moment, our life path comes flooding in from the heavens, through our mothers, and into the crowns of our babies for them to access as and when they need it.

So much about sacred birthing has been lost to us, including sacred conception, and often more than not we are born into trauma from the moment our mothers conceive right through.

I do not say this to shame or deny the gift and beauty of our lives, only to bring that thought to life to land within you, us, the world. There is so much more to all this miraculous divine human experience than we know, and it begins right at our moment of conception through to being crowned at birth with all the wisdom we need to fulfill our life path. In this moment it is not unusual for a mother to suddenly not know her child's name and need some time and space, maybe weeks for the wisdom to fully land, or to change the name in that moment from one that was chosen. I imagine if we were conceived and birthed to the beat of the drum with our name sung soulfully into the hearts of our beings from the moment we arrive, many of us would walk differently in and through our lives. We would walk taller, more certain of the miracle we are, more fully anchored into Earth itself, purposeful and at ease with the gifts we hold. I sing my children's names to them now and have done since they were babies. I recall with ease and, on reflection as I write, it was clearly a knowing within me that each child carries a soul song that they need to hear.

I would make up words for each child, a song of their own. With my sixth babe, Sophia-Rose, I sung her name into her heart. I would find myself singing in sounds and a language not quite known by me yet sung with a knowing that she knows it. Words that would flow with ease would sing life to my children that they were the Earth; the stars; the waters that flowed in every ocean, lake, and river; the roots of every tree and the strength of every trunk and branch; the shine of every star; and sound of every birdsong. I would spend time imagining each child in their place upon the Earth and pray I had the wisdom to let them breathe easy into expressing themselves and living life to the beat of their own drum.

This is often the hardest part as a parent, to create space for our children to take up space in their lives. It's still a prayer I speak.

Chapter Six

Womb Wisdom

&

Light Work

I would not have always had the gnosis to be present to my body, never mind my womb. In fact, I did not give my womb much thought or consideration until I found myself pregnant at 20. Even though pregnant with life, and the transformation was immense, I was still not attuned to its wisdom. It would not be until 2011. I would begin to feel womb whisperings stir awake and I was able to hear what she was saying.

I was moving through so much in those years, working closely with the Angelic realm. For the entirety of 2011, I was working on a map the Archangels gifted me, through guided prayer, ceremony, and daily devotion.

This map represented a different part of the Earth itself. My instruction was that diamond light codes were moving into the planet to prepare it energetically to receive the incoming 2012 crystalline energy.

2011 to 2012 was a huge year in terms of our evolution and the awakening of masses. There were those that felt Christ himself was going to reincarnate upon the Earth. From my understanding, it was not Christ as a human that was arriving upon the Earth but the frequency he mastered in this life and carried within.

I was painting often, and I was meditating a lot. I was alone most days whilst my children were at school. I was listening to my spirit team and guides, and so much was unfolding. I was channelling information daily at this point and this map moved through me. It was honestly sketched so quickly, quite rudimentary, and to anyone looking it would not look like much. Yet, the information that flowed from me, referencing different countries in the world, different gateways of activation, the Archangels that were over seeing each gateway, every symbol was gifted alongside prayers and hand movements. I was in that moment downloading an entire energetic healing gift to support us through our evolution.

I was called upon on the 1.11.11 through to the 11.11.11 at 11.11 am and pm to a devotional practice. I would light candles, place them upon each gateway, speak aloud the prayers, and feel these diamond light codes enter the Earth. I was shown how this light rooted into her and rose through us and our bodies, like electric currents preparing for the momentous changes that would be coming, that are coming, that are here.

On the lead up to the 21-11-11, I was instructed to move into this daily. I was seeing the ways this was assisting not only our planet but humanity.

Years later, I was brought back to this energy and shown how it applied directly to our bodies with a knowing I would bring it to life when fully guided. I have brought the prayers to people and shared the symbols.

I have not yet fully moved it out into the world as the instruction has not been given. I am aware how this sounds as I am writing these words. I am aware you may be reading these words and may find them hard to believe or understand even.

I am aware you may be reading and wanting to know when you can access these teachings. It is not easy to share so much of my journey in this way when I have no idea who will read the words and how they will be responded to.

These words speak truth of my experience and what was asked of me at that time. I do not believe that I am special nor chosen. I do believe that we have each chosen our part at this time as we evolve and take our rightful place within the universe.

I do believe that this small piece I was given to hold as part of my service, gifted something real and loving into the Earth and us all. At this time, my dreams were vivid. I was often in dream time, moving across the Earth and lifting darkness out from her. I was filling these spaces with a frequency of love, just like the love I felt and attempted to describe earlier when sharing about my moment of sacred remembrance and the huge shift in this life.

This work, the map, the prayers, and invocations felt purposeful, loving, necessary even, and I trust that the world over at this time that there were so many souls like me doing similar. Together we were weaving into the Earth gridlines a diamond template that would and could hold the rapid incoming frequencies that are forever changing our world.

I remember at this time asking for support in human form to help me understand this journey that was beginning to feel like something out of a sci-fi movie. I stumbled upon a woman who would impact my life in ways I am still integrating into fullness. This woman is Anaiya Sophia, now known as Alethia Sophia. I saw her speak live through a friend's timeline on the sacred world wide web of Facebook. It is funny- I did not join social media until 2009; I was one of the last of my family and peers. It is also funny how it has played a pivotal role in bringing me to soul mentors and soul sisters. I listened to this woman speak and could feel every part of my body vibrate with a knowing that I was to journey with her. At this time, I was not earning a lot of my own money and there was an offering she had put out into the world, with the option to offer a donation. I wrote to her and asked if I could donate a painting and she replied in the affirmative. She shared with me that she would place it within a chapel dedicated to Mary Magdalene in France. The painting was of the maiden, mother, and crone energy, it was a sacred trinity soul retrieval art piece. Work I am still actively in always.

I would love to offer you a little wisdom to help you understand this energy and work and why it is important divine human work.

What is Maiden, Mother and Crone energy?

- Maiden ~ This energy is of hope, adventure, renewal, youthfulness, playfulness, joy, and trust.

- Mother ~ This energy brings us to our radiance, and our commitments. It explores what we are building, our foundations, and it is creation energy.
- Crone ~ This energy opens our wisdom. It's about knowledge, releasing and rebirthing, coming home to our power, and asks of us devotion.

It makes sense to explore these archetypes in our lives, their light and shadow qualities, gifts, and wounds to gift us an awareness of how each archetype is playing out in our lives and relationships. For in doing so we reach into places on the inside that gift us clarity, direction and confidence and ease in our lives.

What are the shadow energies of these archetypes?

- Maiden ~ lacks commitment, can be cruel in word and intention, relies on her external beauty for validation, and avoids deeper intimacy and life itself.
- Mother ~ Wallows in victimhood, despair, and hurts. Uses manipulation tactics to get her desired outcome in life. Can be attention seeking, harbours resentments and has low self-esteem.
- Crone ~ Overpowers others and uses fear as a motivator. Manipulates her way through life and stays within the logic and intellect of the mind. Is unable to access her bodily wisdom, as she has real disconnection from her body.

Note: Shadow work is not intended to shame, only to bring a new level of awareness about what is playing out in your life, so that you may access the light of its gift.

Our exchange was agreed upon and she sent me the audios, prayers, and ritual I was to participate in. It was over a 21day period and my first introduction to kundalini yoga.

I committed to the journey alongside the soul work shared above, yet this energy felt different to me. I was always up high, yet this energy, this woman, and this work was bringing me down, into my body, into my womb, into my sacral and root like nothing I had ever experienced before.

My spine tingled and felt like it opened. My body arched, my breath shifted, and my heart opened. Orgasmic energy moved through me continuously, yet it was not sexual; it was life giving. I was continuously brought back to my womb.

My hands would rest upon my belly and womb, and I would just breathe with her.

I started to receive multiple visions of me priestessing, in ceremony, ritual, and prayer. I could feel its power and urgency wanting to arrive in the space with me. It felt like another soul piece coming to life, another expression of my expanded state coming to greet me. I suddenly found myself aching for the mother of all Mothers.

I was seeing the faces of the mother, many of whom I did not recognise, for in this lifetime I did not know the face of the mother, only my own, Mother Mary, and some female saints through my Catholic upbringing.

The one that called me the most at this time was Mary Magdalene, Hathor and the Dark Mother. I had some knowing of Mary Magdalene and had felt her close with me as early as 15 years of age, yet had no real understanding of who she really was. Only a deep knowing in my bones that it wasn't what I heard in chapel through the word of man. That I knew. Without knowing how, I knew I just did. I did not know the face of the dark Mother nor Hathor, yet I knew them and recognised them both within my heart.

A soul gift – A practice for discernment – knowing if a soul guide is of the highest love and intention within your energetic field.

- Close your eyes
- Feel the sensation of your in breath and out breath
- Feel your connection to your heart energy and feel it open
- Call forth your soul guide you know is connecting with you
- Ask it – "What is your connection to me?"
- Ask it "What is your intention?"
- Ask it "Are you of the highest love and vibration?"
- Ask it "Do you mean me harm?"

Universal law states that all energy must reveal its true intention. If you feel an energy with you that does not feel invited or consented to, ask it to leave or make its intention known to you in a way you can fully receive, so that you understand its presence in your life. Anything that is not of love must leave upon your request.

In quiet moments, I would feel a grief well up inside of me, an ache for woman, for the feminine wisdom, for something lost, yet I had no real idea what was lost to me. I knew through this experience, these memories, these longings, aches, and desires that it lived in my sacral. That my womb was seeking to be remembered. This energy could very easily be mistaken for and did feel like sexual energy, only it was not an energy that was to be used for sex. This energy was asking something different of me.

My human mind was grappling with the unknown. My soul was dancing with delight as this remembrance rooted into my being for more of my life to unravel, all the while I was still as ordinary as the day was long. Still a mother. Still a wife. Still a daughter. A friend.

A woman living what felt like two separate lives with no understanding how to merge the two. Who was I becoming? Who would understand me? Where was this path taking me?

Why did I feel compelled to share and instinctively knew what to withhold?

This drop into my body, into my womb, into the belly of my own innate power and presence, was the beginning of my descent into the underworld of my own existence to meet what was hard and face with love where possible.

I will tell you now 2012 and all that crystalline light was not an easy transition nor integration for many- myself included.

So much was asked of us all.

Chapter Seven
The Whispers

This descent into my body, into my womb, was an invitation to really get intimate with my body temple, my messiness, my humanness, and my inner wisdom in ways I had not met before. I was meeting sisters of the heart increasingly and soon was regularly circling with some. One of which brought me to a circle to connect deeper with our wombs wisdom.

This circle was a life changing experience for me. Here I was in circle with a woman teaching about the power of our wombs, and how deepening into our cyclical nature as a woman was a key part in reclaiming our innate power as women. I at this point was regularly laying my hands upon her (my womb) and speaking to her, yet I had not thought about the importance or the value of paying attention to my cycle to understand myself on an emotional, mental, physical, sexual, and spiritual level.

As she spoke, and I dropped into her wisdom and soon after her books (which I will reference at the end of this book), I was totally inspired and empowered by what my own body temple could lead me to. I was aware of chakras, I was aware of energy, and I was aware of sacred prayer and ritual. I was starting to open and flourish in my life.

Mary Magdalene was regularly whispering into my heart rituals of devotion. I was beginning to really understand and have an awareness of the wisdom that my body held and desired for me to know. It was fascinating and infuriating all at once.

Questions like-

- Why is this information not readily available to every teen girl?
- Why is this information hidden?
- Why is there is so much shame around our menstrual cycles?
- Why have I carried so much shame around being a woman in this world?

I would love to invite you into a practice that has stayed with me and directed my life path of devotion daily since it was first brought to me.

Soul guidance on how to honour your cyclical nature.

- Purchase a Journal
- On day one of your bleed, pay attention to how you are feeling emotionally, mentally, physically, spiritually, and sexually.
- If you no longer bleed, use the new moon as your day one right through to the full moon.
- Reflect upon how you respond or react to life, with a focus on your relationships to yourself, others, food, and work/ business.
- Do this consistently for a 3-month cycle and you will notice patterns begin to emerge.

Reflective questions to support this journey.

1. How did you feel mentally today?
2. How did you feel emotionally today?
3. How did you feel in your body?
4. How do you feel energetically?
5. How reactive were you today? 6. How creative were you today?
6. How well did you eat?
7. How responsive were you to touch, affection and love today?
8. How focused were you on tasks you had planned today?
9. How did you sleep last night?
10. How connected did you feel to your heart and soul practices?
11. How did you feel around people today?

These reflective questions, when committed to in a consistent way, can bring your life into so much sacred balance. You will not burn out and instead feel empowered and connected to your energy source from within. These patterns will reveal to you key information about how you are doing in life. You will notice the days when you will be feeling-

- Most energised, and excited about life, people, and your work.
- More vulnerable, tired, and in need of extra buffering and TLC.
- When you are most honest, and able to have the hard conversations.
- Most creative, and able to hold he energy of certain projects in your life.
- More able to hold more and when it is best you have a duvet day.

4 benefits of working with your cyclical rhythms

- Finding better balance.
- Creating supportive systems in your life.
- Ensures that you are using your energy wisely.
- Avoid burn out.

This entire book was written on the cusp of my bleed, which shifted throughout the writing of this book. It has started to shift due to being peri menopausal. So, I am leaning into this practice so much right now to grasp my ever-changing ebbs and flows. The forties have been an interesting ride thus far! Most of these words were written on the Balsamic Moon, also known as the Dark Moon, which arrives around 3 and half days before the New Moon. When I tried to force my writing, nothing would come. I simply had to wait and honour my cycle of creativity which flows better on the cusp of my day one.

This invitation to pay attention to my cyclical nature gifted me a different level of depth with my being. It was a new way of being present, and an ability to sharpen my abilities to attune to what I really wanted and needed in life. To feel fulfilled, loved, held, and met, and still I was stumbling and relearning so much about how I could live, laugh and love more in this life.

I was changing rapidly in these years. I recall a particular shift in my marriage- in the way that I held myself within it, as well as the way that I spoke and desired to be spoken to. I have vivid memory of Seamus and I in a tense moment, and on reflection I am sure he was looking from the outside wondering who is this woman, who is she becoming?

I know I was feeling this for myself. In many ways I was unrecognisable, yet much of the same. I like to say to the women who have trusted me to hold them for a moment on their path this soul whispering truth.

A soul whisper ~ Remember this

"You will leave me different yet more of yourself than ever before."

In this moment of in-between tension where all that was, was being held by all that desired to come to life, he said, "You have changed, I don't know who you are anymore."

I replied to him, "Yes, I have changed and grown, and now we either grow together or grow apart."

Admittedly it may not have been so polite or contained. The energy of change was intense and strong, as was this exchange between us!

It is often the people we love the most who struggle with how rapidly we change on this path of remembrance. Extending some grace their way is important too.

Recognising when it is time to let go is also important.

Sadly, not everyone gets to walk the whole path home with us.

I knew who I was becoming needed space and room to expand in whatever direction my energy needed to flow. I needed to know he could hold it, me, and us alongside me.

Women on this path are not easy women to journey with, for we will call those walking with us into the depths of their own being, into what is being left unsaid and unmet. It is why we are the way we are. We are here to live and love differently than this world remembers right now. We are the remembrance, the soul whispers for humanity.

I felt strongly within me that nothing could shift my direction backwards. I was being stretched; we all were. Life was, and collectively we all were too. I wrote this piece many years later, it feels like it belongs right here with us now.

SHE whispers

"Humanity is currently witnessing its own rot in the underbelly of its own shadow. As we are squeezed so tightly that the pus oozes out of the deep wounds of our own creation and it is painful. To witness the horrors of humanity. The horrors of what we humans are capable of and what we do to one another. It is very real. Not an illusion. This dark is real. It happens. Every day in our lives. Denying the ego is part of the problem. Trying to dismantle the ego without first recognising its purpose and gift is part of the poison that keeps feeding the monster. Many feel and fear the world is falling apart. It is not. It is not breaking down. It is breaking through the unsustainable, unhealthy, and unholy ways in which we have chosen to live and exist on this planet. Many back in 2012 were called into their own darkness as the light amplified and anchored into the Earth like never before, leading those that heard that call to love in the previous years into the underbelly of their own humanity – shadow. Those that answered the call came home to themselves through this intense fire blazing initiation. They are now rising brighter and fuller in joy with a true level of compassion, empathy, love, awareness, and wisdom that is both ancient and new. These ancients can and will create safety for those facing the reality of their own undercurrents at present. There is no fast track through the underbelly of our own shadow. Alone or collectively. It must be faced. There is no attunement, light code, or transmission that will lift you up and out. Meeting thyself is what will lift you up and out."

Coming home to the wisdom of my womb brought me home to a path I had a whisper of in 2000.

In 2009 I was in the garden meditating. My feet were firmly upon the ground, my heart open. I was breathing and moving my body intuitively. I was never truly taught how to be with my body, yet this wisdom began to pour through with the guidance of the Angels. They often shared with me the importance of recognising that as much as we were soul, we were human- divinely human.

To be ashamed of or even deny our humanness was to deny how sacredly made we are. I have often felt and spoken to the belief that if we were truly to ascend, we first need to descend and master our humanity in order to integrate it fully with our soul's energy. It is a fool's game to try to deny the very real fact that we are here in a human body.

If we were to assist only from the higher realms, we would not be in a body here on Earth. We have chosen this time to incarnate, to learn the art of sacred embodiment. To be both holy and human.

To meet the polarity of our existence with compassion and acceptance. We come here to experience an Earthly life, a life of relationship in the mind, body, and heart. We cannot do that if we are constantly shaming our humanness and trying to escape it.

We receive the higher wisdom so that we can integrate it into our human lives and call forth the energy of Eden (I believe this to be the feminine principle that is seeking expression upon our planet right now) into our everyday living. This is what makes this human experience one of the most sought-after experiences in the Universe.

On this day I was referring to in 2009, I was experiencing the fullness of what it was to be in my body and recall a soul memory. This memory made no sense to me, even though at the time it also felt like home.

I was in a temple with two other priestesses we were robed in white and looked to me as though we were celebrating the sun through a ritual dance. As this memory landed into my body, I knew it was important. However, it was not until years later as I was moving deeper into the wisdom of my womb through the wisdom of the Goddess and her many faces, did this vision make sense to me.

I did not know what a priestess was back then, nor did I know of any feminine face of God other than Mother Mary to pray to and lean into. As I deepened into working with my womb, I began to get truly clear visions of my life as a priestess and its role in this lifetime. I began to create sacred space for personal prayer and devotion calling upon the wisdom of the Mother of all Mothers.

The Holy Sophia: I never in my life felt an ache like I did for the feminine. It felt like grief, rage, and longing to return to her to the wisdom of my own beating heart and the truest pulse of my womb. I was being inspired by the women around me, I was circling regularly with sisters of the heart. Each of us were learning the art of holding space and each other in conscious loving ways. Little did I know I was doing the groundwork for holding space, holding the women who felt called to sit with me in the years that would follow.

A soul whisper ~ Remember this

"To hold space is to hold a divine human where they are."

What does it mean to hold space?

It means we hold space …

- With no desire to fix
- With no desire to offer advice unless invited to do so
- With no desire to make another wrong
- With no judgement
- With no pressure for another to find a solution
- With an awareness that many never get to simply speak and share their truths without interruption from life, partners, children, or other responsibilities
- With the wisdom to know that we each holds our own codes of remembrance safe within our bodies, and when our bodies feel safe, we will open and reclaim what has always been ours all along.

A soul whisper ~ Remember this

"To hold space is an honour, a gift, it is something that humbles you time and time again and opens reverence for us divine humans and all that we hold."

I have the belief from my experiences that women hold within them the feminine key codes of sacred remembrance. They are uniquely her own, whispered into what she is made of- which is heavenly stardust, blood, and bones. We remember within our bones a time when temples fell. We know how the divine mother of creation held our power, our wisdom, our secrets and whispered them into the bones of our existence, the lands, the rivers, the rocks, the heavens above, for us to recall and call home to the heart of our consciousness when the time is right. I believe that time to be now.

I believe that women the world over are hearing her call and are being stirred awake through the body and sisterhood the world over. If you are reading these words, you know and feel this too, even if you have not grasped the enormity of this gift and miracle of our times.

In a recent dream, as I visited the sacred heart of Avalon, I dreamt of many Magdalene sisters of the Rose in Egypt who were robed in red, pulling darkness up from the sacred portals that exist there and placing down into them golden light codes. They were reactivating the land itself, dissolving all dark magic that has been affecting our consciousness' for some time.

I knew in this dream we were collectively working together on this path home to restoring Gaia to her rightful place within the Universe. Women are finding themselves being called upon to assist and help in ways that make little to no logical sense to those not yet aware of the evolutionary times we are in.

Womb work became about clearing pathways within me that I did not know existed.

Womb work became about reclaiming lost knowledge that every woman needs in her life.

Womb work became a whole new path of integration on this holy human life and activated within me a strong desire to share what I was learning. It started as a personal journey to descend into my body, shame free, and untangle myself from the wounding of the sexual trauma. It became a way of living and purpose that has served and continues to serve so many beyond me. It is to this moment, one of the deepest and most profound journeys I have taken and continue to walk to this day.

These words moved through me after a womb and throat activation. May they call home something of value to you now in this moment.

Womb Wisdom speaks I walk with you now Opening doors. Activating Memories. Igniting Passions and purpose. Lifting veils of confusion and doubt. Feeling deep the ways of old.

Roaring our whispered stories once afraid to be told. Burning through our veins. Running through our blood. Blood to the earth. Blessings of SHE

You. I. We. That came to be

Mother of the Earth. I feel you there. Strong. Rooted. Connected. A part of me.

Holding. Strengthening. Grounding. Guiding. Anchoring. Building Foundations upon which we stand. Thank you, thank you, Thank you. Mother of love. May we know you

May we know you have not abandoned us in our hour of need. For I know you have not left me. For in my eyes, you reflect that which I need to see

You reflect the soul of my truth. The Akashic whisperers of wisdom. The miracle way of being. Love, love, love. Is what you ask of us.

Hold the child. Innocence protects. Anoint with love. Forever more. Dance child dance. Sing child. Joyous, Ecstatic Expression must be seen to be met by those yet to feel

Let go my child

Breathe, Breathe, Breathe

Into Life. Into Love. Feel it. Be it. See it. Meet it. Love it

For you are all of it

Sacred, Holy, Human, Divine Perfection- no part can be forever held back from the love that exists because you exist."

A Soul Gift ~ A ritual of devotion to support your connection to your womb wisdom.

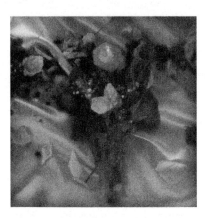

Womb Mandala

What you need: Something that represents each element:

Earth, Water, Fire, Air - Choose what you feel most aligned to

- Flowers ~ Fresh & Dried – I like to use roses from my garden or bought fresh. I also used dried petals that have been used in sacred ceremony for several years now that I add to after each ritual of devotion.
- Shells
- Stones and pebbles
- Twigs and fallen leaves
- Crystals

A play list that drops you into your feminine power

- Candles

- Scarf or fabric that you would like to use in a ritual – I have different scarves for different rituals
- A bowl of holy waters

Choose a day that feels significant and sacred to you.

Examples of sacred days and energy to explore with focused intention and devotion

- Venus Day – Fridays – The day of the Goddess – Devotion – Self-love and care - Your favourite moon phase:
1. New moon – new beginnings – setting sacred intention – planting seeds
2. Waxing crescent moon- visualising – acting towards positive transformations
3. First Quarter – reflection- meeting challenges – a time to work towards your goals
4. Waxing Gibbous – commitment – patience – dedication – protection
5. Full Moon – celebration – abundant – completion – honour your growth
6. Waning Gibbous – receive and give – releasing – The energy of gratitude
7. Last Quarter – forgiveness – grace – compassion
8. Waning Crescent – endings – reflection – working with your intuition – resetting personal goals.

The day of your first bleed

Your ovulation day, if working with the energy of conception

This is a very simple yet powerful ritual of devotion. It invites you to work with your own intuitive wisdom and move into what feels aligned for you. I do these both indoors and outdoors. I will share a way to do both.

Here are my suggestions for you.

- Create space for yourself
- Create a sacred space if indoors – soft candlelight – music that brings you to that place on the inside where you know and trust yourself
- Bless every item you intend to use – I hold it in my hands and pray into it – I use prayer in accordance with my intention for the ritual.
- Lay down your scarf – I work as close to the Earth as possible – if indoors, I am on the floor – if outdoors, I am bare footed on my knees.
- Begin by placing something in the centre of your mandala – to represent you and your sacred prayer for the healing you are bringing to life
- Begin to build the mandala out from that place adding in your items. You can move through the directions to create a sacred holding for the energy within the centre.
- All the while you are calling on your soul support
- You are using your soul energy to infuse the mandala
- You anoint yourself and the mandala when complete with the holy waters
- You light each candle and speak your prayer out loud
- You place your hands upon your heart and your womb
- Rest your hands upon your womb, thumbs touching and fingers pointing downwards- a womb mudra - feel your hands being energised by her, by your womb wisdom.
- You then move your hands up over your belly, and heart, then turn the hands outwards up towards the throat, third eye and towards the heavens.
- Connect with a Goddess of your choosing – I work with Hathor, Isis, Mary Magdalene, Bridget, Sekhmet, Kali, Mother Mary, and Quan Yin, to name a few.
- Bring the energy back down and fill the womb mandala with this sacred energy by moving your hands over it.

- Let these candles burn and rest into presence – pay attention to any visuals – messages – gnosis you receive and journal on that.

I leave these womb Mandalas for 3 days and tend to them daily, this ritual of devotion supports you into coming home to a part of that remembers what it is to live sacredly attuned to what lives and breathes in you. Work with what feels sacred and true for you.

Benefits my soul clients have felt working with these mandalas

- A deeper connection to their bodies
- Confidently speaking their truths
- Clearing deep seated intimacy issues

Softening the pain residue from sexual trauma

- Clearing fertility issues.
- Healing sisterhood wounds
- Healing mother wounds

Working with our womb wisdom invites us into powerfully reclaiming our unique soul song, message and gifts. Activating and inspiring our purpose daily. It helps us reconnect, not only to ourselves but the red thread of love that exists between all women.

The one I have felt most personally is the words my womb whispers to me, my soul voice refined. My inner voice got stronger, as did my sacred remembrance.

Seeding in circles of love started to become a way of living and loving for me. I was opening and becoming more visible on my path, sharing snippets of love wherever possible. Invitations started to open for me to come and create sacred space. I was in England, and it began with Angel circles. I would arrive at the home I was invited to, and we would gather in circle. I would open the space with prayer and intention, before calling upon the Angels and moving through a channelled meditation for those that had joined us. Word spread, sisterhoods were created, friendships were born. I spent months in the home of a dear sister with four others. We would meet every new and full moon and take it in turns to hold sacred space for one another. Each being held and each holding, leaning into our sacred feminine gifts.

A soul whisper ~ Remember this

"If you don't have a women's circle, find one or create one, your life will be forever changed by this experience." What is a women's circle?

A women's circle is a sacred gathering of women that offers her …

- A space to breathe and let go
- A space to lean into trust with sisters of the heart
- A space to grow through her wounds
- A space to deepen her spiritual practice
- A space to integrate her soul's wisdom
- A space where she can be loved, met and held exactly as she is
- A space where she can cry as freely as she laughs
- A space where she can dance and move her body without fear of being shamed or lusted after.
- A space of safety

A woman's circle is a spiral of support that keeps on expanding and calling more women home to the heart of what is true.

Lakota Wisdom

"In the circle we are all equal, there is no one in front of you, no one behind you, there is no one above you, or below you. The circle is sacred because it is designed to create unity."

These circles were the root that all my offerings sprung forth from. For, if I had not had this sacred space to drop into safely, I would not have grown in confidence to believe I had the power, presence and skillset to hold and nurture. These roots were humble yet honest. Filled with love, presence, and integrity. From these roots I grew, expanded, and began to move around and create more offerings. I was leaning into my soul wisdom, angelic knowledge, womb wisdom, creativity, and something bigger than me began to unfurl and arrive.

I recall being out walking and it was a beautiful day. I was feeling deeply connected to my path, yet I had a weariness descend upon me as I walked. I asked God to show me what this weariness was. I was instantly brought to a moment where it felt like I shape shifted and I became old, like older than old, ancient. I felt the first flutter of my first incarnation. I felt myself holding a staff to hold me up energetically and I felt the tiredness of thousands of souls, years, and life on this planet.

I also felt and knew my promise to return always until all humans remembered they too had a soul, a divine counterpart that was seeking to integrate with their divine human part.

I felt the exhaustion from my soul promise and the weariness of being human that felt and knew more than I cared to in that moment. I felt the heaviness of the path of humanity we were opening to. I felt the crossroads and the invitations for us to choose the path of ease, knowing so many of us were not ready.

I could feel and see the hardships yet to be walked in and through. I was given dates of significance, years even- 2012, 2013, 2016, and 2020 to 2024. By 2032 I was shown our world would be unrecognisable for any of us.

That path is still being written by our choices and is not yet clearly defined, yet love is more present than ever before. No matter what the world out there looks like, turn inwards right here, right now with me. Our greatest task right now is to stay in the presence of love, in connection to our higher heart wisdom.

Soul Gift – A heart meditation

- Place your hand upon your heart and close your eyes ☐ Feel the sensation of your in breath and out breath.
- Feel your body weight drop to the floor
- Feel it drop deeper into the Earth beneath your feet
- Feel it drop deeper into the center of the Earth
- Feel yourself strengthened by your connection to her
- Feel the roots wrap around your crystalline center
- Feel this energy move upwards

- Feel this energy rise up through the roots of connection you have just made
- Feel it move up through your feet
- Up through the root – bottom of your spine
- Up through your spine
- Towards the nape of your neck
- Up around the back of your head
- Through the crown of your head
- Connecting to the heavens
- Feel a strong rod of light supporting you energetically
- When you feel this clearly in your field, begin to imagine the energy from the heavens move downwards through the crown, throat and find rest in the heart.
- Imagine at the same time, the energy rising upwards from the centre of the Earth move through the root, into the solar (belly) and into the heart.
- Let yourself sit with this loving energy resting in your heart space for as long as you feel called to
- Practice this daily
- Expand your practice by extending this love outwards into any area of your life or the collective field you feel called to share it with.

Know that this love is real. Know that you can choose it in any given moment. Use and share it wisely!

Remember that love can choose hard things too, that not all hard choices lead to more disconnect.

I have found at times the opposite to be true. An example for me is choosing to leave Ireland felt like a hard choice and it was, but it opened my world in ways that would never have happened had I chosen to stay. Imagine all the incredible humans and love I would have missed.

Imagine all the paintings that would never have been painted. Imagine all the channelled love sitting there waiting for me to choose it. I would not have chosen any of it had I not made the hard choice of leaving my home and family.

It is likely these words would not have made it onto the pages of a book, for so much of what I met would not have happened. The circles of beings I met, loved, and was forever changed by would not have happened. I would not have returned home and began to seed in the circle of love that to this day continues to make spirals of connection that I could never have envisioned back when hard choices became a daily act of self-love.

Humanity is in that place right now where we are being called daily to make what feels like hard choices of love that are forever changing the landscape of our existence upon this Earth.

We are choosing the path of healing, of conscious communication, of deep diving into our ancestral wounding's. We are, for the first time as a humanity, properly aware of the trauma that exists on our planet, and there is a collective wave of awareness that we can move into this with love and compassion for those that came before us so that those who come after us have a path of ease in comparison.

We sacred holy humans need to tread gently through these changing times, so we do not cage ourselves in a perpetual loop of continuous hurting. It helps enormously to consider the magnitude of what we are moving through right now.

Native Americans believe our actions affect seven generations before and after us. With that wisdom in my heart, I have come to believe that we need to understand that there is much we have carried forth that is not ours alone. We have each chosen a particular piece to heal.

I will share a story of that for understanding how this has played out in my life. This is something only few know as I rarely speak to it outside of trusted circles. In this moment of this book, I am inviting you deeper into trust. I am inviting you into circle with me.

It may help to imagine me there with you in circle- candles lit, where our hearts and minds are open so this may be received.

I ask you to feel the words in the body as our body often feels truth in ways our minds struggle to.

So please move forwards into the following words with trust that I am holding you in circle safely.

When I was in my most troubled state growing up, I was finding it difficult to understand what was real and what was not. I was having very vivid flashbacks of an attack with soldiers. It felt so real to me that I shared it with my then counsellor and older brother.

I recall sharing with my older brother on the stairs of our home, trying to make sense of this memory whilst also feeling I was going quite mad and losing my mind rapidly. He, in all his patience and support, just listened.

He is like that, he listens, lets you lean in, does not say much yet you know you are held. This memory felt hard to hold. Life moved on and I moved into more ease in my life and did not give it much thought for years. Fast forward to 2016.

I went to what I call a seer, a woman who sees beyond the veils and brings information back from source. As she read for me, she started to speak about and to a grandmother four generations removed. She described a village being ransacked by soldiers and her being attacked by many of them as they burned down her village. She was 17 years old. This grandmother had a message for me. Her message was this

"The memories I had were hers and that what I was healing in this lifetime began with her and ended with me."

The seer continued to speak to me and offered me guidance on my daughters, the pieces they were holding, and what I could do to lessen the burden for them in this lifetime. I cried as she spoke to me as I felt the pain of my lineage, the memories of old, and the hope of future. It all made sense.

All of it made sense. When I was 17 years old, seeing and fearing much with little to no understanding of the hidden realms of existence that are alive upon this Earth plane. These years of sacred remembrance are snippets of my soul's wisdom returned slowly over time to integrate. Gifting me an understanding about what was happening to me at that pivotal time in my life.

We live in a world here in the west that shames the wise ones, which classifies those of us who see beyond this veil as insane. That has forgotten how to hold and honour its most sacred: the feminine, the seers, who come here from beyond the stars with information and gifts to access the worlds secrets to guide us.

I knew in this connection all those years later that what I moved through in those previous vulnerable years was very much an initiation activating within me. Which was a remembrance of what lived in me and what was possible.

I didn't have an elder with soul wisdom who could hold me in the ways I needed, no guide or no teacher, of these matters.

I often wonder if I had how different it may have been.

Yet, I also have a strong knowing it was exactly as I had chosen it to be before I came Earth side. My initiations in this lifetime come thick and fast. Sometimes I rarely get a moment to catch my breath. I asked the Angels once why this was? They said I came this time knowing I had less time to do what I came here to do! So, I chose a fast-track through humanities pain points which left me feeling about 101 by the time I was 21.

I share this story to gift you something to reach into with regards to the generational impact and healing that can occur seven generations back and forwards.

With this knowledge, you can now be aware and pay attention to the patterns and pieces in your life on repeat and begin to get ever more curious about why it's present. Soul gift - A way to work with your ancestry.

- Reflect upon your mother and fathers' journey
- Ask about their parents and their journeys
- If possible, go back as far as you can
- Bring the pieces of the story together
- Bring awareness to their strengths and traumas.
- Feel into your experience of them, the impact they had on you
- Explore ways to find compassion for them, for you, for everyone.
- Explore the patterns on repeat within your ancestry
- Explore the ways you are repeating these patterns
- Feel into one you would like to shift and clear
- Seek mentorship, council, energetic support if needed to work with this piece of the story
- If you feel able to do it alone, find ways to honour the story, the ones who came before and celebrate their part in your story.

Create ceremony to release what you are no longer willing to carry forwards – a simple effective ceremony is to write down what you wish to release and burn it.

What is one part you can take into your heart and choose differently to shift the trajectory of experiences for those behind and in front of you?

Own it and breathe loving acceptance into it. Create space to get curious about what it's true gift is. I have no doubt in my heart that all we try to avoid, deny, repress, and ignore gets increasingly insistent that we look at it, eye to eye, heart to heart, and face to face with all that lives in us so we soften into its gift.

The path of awareness is not a path everyone wants to walk, as it requires skilful inner work where we begin the art of dissecting and exploring the stories and experiences brought to life on our journey.

We unravel and dive into the dark spaces within to witness more fully the ways in which our stories play out in our lives.

It is not for the faint of heart as we begin to get real about what is true and what is holding us back from witnessing the truth. It gifts us the ability to move forwards in life with a little more grace as we whittle our way through the endless rabbit holes within the mind that separate us from love.

We begin to see through clearer eyes how the mind can become rigidly fixed and attached to certain stories, and the impact this is having on us. We see the invitation to begin a process of letting go of versions of our reality that no longer resonate with the truth of who we are.

I feel this journey inwards a constant creator of a greater sense of purpose, wellness, and wholeness. This is, in my view, a conscious journey into the shadow personality that lives within us all. An opportunity to meet the parts of us we have judged as less than, shamed, and been afraid to meet.

We become less afraid of what once felt difficult, and more open to meeting inner discomfort with a knowing that we can now unravel the fear, judgements, and pain we have held so tightly to.

These moments require us to seek soft landings and fierce loving holding from not only ourselves but those we trust. It becomes a gift of space, time, and self-care so we can dissolve the inner pain and stories into inner love stories. Where compassion becomes the one leading us into acceptance.

What I came to meet in this space of my journey and continue to meet is an understanding from deep within my bones that there is no part of me that cannot be met with love, no part.

I rise into that knowing repeatedly and it helps hold me in the face of the drama trauma loop so many of us humans are attached to. We learn to embody what I call the 3 R's- a little soul practice gifted to me by the Angels once upon a time.

I was painting an oracle deck Angel Whispers at the time. I was holding and managing life, motherhood and I was heavily pregnant. My tolerance for others was low and I recall this loving soul practice arriving in to gift me spaciousness to meet life a little slower and lovingly.

Chapter Eight

Retreat

Rethink

Respond

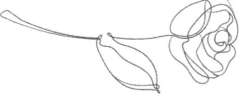

What are the 3 R's?

Retreat, Rethink, Respond, ... honestly, these 3 little Rs gifted me and those I loved much grace when often I truly wanted to bulldoze through life and some of what was showing up for me to walk in and through.

I invite you to try this little snippet of soul wisdom in your life, particularly when you are holding life heavier than normal. It is akin to what I now often call a sacred pause. It gives us a moment to really meet what is present without an over-reaction that may create cause or bring more harm and hurt.

It gifts us space to begin to understand that we often cannot control what is going on outside of us, yet we have the power and ability to control how we respond to life. It is a powerful soul tool to bring love into the room, knowing it is always present.

How do they work?

- Retreat- take space.
- Rethink- what is the best course of action right now?
- Respond- can my response be from my heart and not my pain?

This simple effective soul tool helps my sometimes impatient and not always so gentle human-self navigate tricky emotions, people, and experiences repeatedly.

It came at a time in my life when it mattered. I share this with many of the people I mentor and offer them this golden nugget to take with them wherever life wants to take them.

Many report back repeatedly how helpful it is. I hope it is for you too.

I will say too it takes courage to take the journey inwards into the unpleasant parts of our personality and really love ourselves there.

It takes a certain awareness to catch ourselves in the reaction in order to first retreat. It sounds simple, yet it can take practice and deep belly breaths as you shift from a state of reactionary impulsiveness. This has often formed in our psyche for a reason that is valid.

I want to share with you a piece of writing in a moment that I wrote when I was moving into the underbelly of my own rage. I found this the hardest part of myself to reach into and love. I sometimes still do!

In the 3 R's I was often slowed down enough to meet a part of me I found hard to meet and love. That part of me that was angry, defensive, unable to feel safe and offer her some respite from years of needing to protect me from the plentiful harmful spaces and places my life met.

I recall the time I moved into this part of my psyche well. I was shocked by her wildness and rage at my refusal to meet her inside of me. She was gnarly and unforgiving and it felt like I walked into the lion's den to be eaten alive, and there was nothing I could do but surrender. At the time, I could not hold myself with the tenderness needed. I do now and dropped into this work safely with trusted sisters at the time. I honestly do not believe we can rise into a compassionate, loving space within without meeting these parts which we shun and shame. Shame loves to hide, loves secrets and hidden places. Shadow work to me is lifting shame up close into the softest place I have available in my heart so I can hold it with the tenderness it's always deserved. If you are someone who has experienced pain and trauma as a child, shame will be hiding in the most unlikely spaces within and around, and you. Begging you to hold her in love. I strongly encourage those of you in this work taking the deep dives underwater to have solid trusted people around you that can be both a soft landing and fierce holder of space, as well as accountability, as it will serve you well. I am blessed to have such incredible divine humans and mentors in my life.

The words that follow may rise you in compassion or judgement. Neither is right nor wrong; it simply is what is being met in you as you read on. It may be particularly hard for anyone who has a fixed impression of who I am.

For now, I invite you to witness and drop into those parts that may too live in you with love, compassion, and grace. Know that I live to explore deeply all that I am so that I can hold others in all that they are. It is what makes circling with me so powerful. For us to absolutely love ourselves, we must know thyself. Nothing gets left out in the dark. I call it all home to love where possible and if I can't do it alone, I call upon those I know to hold me in love to guide me back to that place that knows love lives here always. By here, I mean inside of me. I have direct constant reach to that truth always.

The shadow of my rage speaks…

"There is a cruelty in me. She rises out of my tongue harshly with little or no remorse. Hard faced. Angry. Snarky. Vengeful. Spiteful. Violent in words and sometimes actions.

My body tenses in her presence. My face contorts into something unrecognisable to me. There is no way to control her. Whilst her presence is less so these days, she is still there begging for a homecoming. A welcomed seat at the table. With so much love in my heart, I find it hard to accept that such cruelty can co-exist inside of me; yet it does. It is real. It is mine.

It is as much a part of me as the expression of love, compassion and grace is. It exists in you too. Maybe not? I imagine we all have a gnarly part of us roaming on the outskirts of our being, seeking refuge with the parts we deem as more acceptable. For me, she has spilled out from inside of me. From the underbelly of my pain. Clawing her way out of the dark corners I pushed her into repeatedly to look me in the eye. I want to look away, only I cannot as she is spilling out everywhere. Into my relationships. Often in the strangest of moments. Unprovoked. Yet something has provoked her.

A red mist descends and up she rises with an intense heat filling my heart, pouring out a fire in my words that would burn through the toughest exterior.

My mother has met her.

My father has too,

My siblings have known her.

My children have caught glimpses of her.

I have met her outside of myself also through the frustrations and actions of those I love. Through a teacher's insensitive offloading. In immature friendships. In women's circles.

Children's playgrounds. Traffic jams. Shop queues. The impatient mother. In my own children. She is present in us all to varying degrees.

This cruel part of me fills the softer parts of me with fear. Shame and guilt too. She feels powerful. All consuming. The more I suppress her, the more she fights to be seen. As she powerfully twists and turns up the burning inside of me, I squirm uncomfortable in her presence. I can see behind the venom spitting from her foaming mouth, a deep longing to be safe, seen, heard, and held. She is hurting, angry, so incredibly sad. She looks out into this world through my eyes, seeing only pain. With a desire to grasp all beings with a ferocity that shakes them into action, and to shift out of the pain body we have become so accustomed and addicted to being in. I was not always conscious of her presence inside of me. I got curious about when this energy and expression were born in me. Was she born in me? Or did she birth to protect a part of me that could not protect itself? "

This curiosity opened a level of compassion I was unable to extend towards this part of myself ever before. I got to explore this part of me without the incessant need to beat myself up. This golden thread of curiosity became a lifeline, a way in, a doorway for her to walk through so she could finally take a seat at the table. A way to greet her and create a soft spot for her to fall into. A place of safety on the inside where she is no longer shunned in shame by the righteousness of a superiority in me that could not extend love for its judgement was so harsh.

How do we do this work?

There is a practice I was moved into some time ago that I have found most effective for reaching into the gift of our painful feelings and/or experiences. It is one I lean into and use regularly with my soul clients.

Soul Gift – A somatic practice for guiding us into the gift of love our pain wishes for us to receive.

- Close your eyes.
- Drop into the sensation of your in breath and out breath
- Move slowly into the body.
- Recall the hurt, the painful experience, or feeling that has felt hard of late.
- Feel into the body and ask the body to show you where this hurt lives.
- When you locate where it is, see if you can experience the sensation of this feeling
- Feel into its colour, texture, shape, form, gathering up as much information and detail as you can.
- When you have a clear sense of where it is, what it looks and feels like- Validate it ~ affirm "I feel you (Name the where in the body) I see you (Describe what it looks like) I feel you (Describe what it feels like, its colour, texture, and sensation)

- Witness how it responds to your validation
- Now let's take it a step further – Ask it aloud "What do you need to feel safe and loved right now?"
- Wait for its answer
- Validate its answer by speaking aloud "I am hearing you need (state what it expressed it needed)
- Pay attention to how it responds and changes every time you validate what is happening within.
- Continue to validate with statements like

  1. I see …
  2. I hear …
  3. I feel …

- Continue with this practice until you feel the gift of its medicine

Some examples of what has shifted for people who have received this soul medicine from working with me

- Pain into Calm
- Tension into Joy
- Scarcity into Freedom
- Restriction into Self-belief
- Grief into relief
- Hurt into Playfulness

All report a feeling of expansion, a lighter feeling in their bodies, aches and pains leaving their bodies, and a feeling of peace enveloping them. One woman reporting at the age of 63 that it was the first time she ever felt fully in her own body and how joyful it felt for her. Our bodies are messengers of the highest order and only desire for us to be in our highest possible state of being. Our aches, pains and hurts are guides into more love for ourselves.

Moving into this part of myself, my rage and others like it gifted me a softening in my belly, as well as the spaciousness to exhale and really recognise what felt like a truth I had not met before.

Which is that we cannot heal this planet, our relationships with ourselves, our families, our lives, and/or each other, if we continue to deny the parts of ourselves that are uncomfortable and harder to love.

What I share in these pages is the journey and processes I was and continue to be invited into. I was opened to the love that is real and that lives in us all in 2009 so that I could meet all that was real and hard to love inside of me.

This is what true remembrance is. This is the path of wholeness. This is the way of love. It is not about seeking, releasing, or even healing. It is for me more about coming home to the heart of our beings. To love, to compassion, to acceptance. In this we dissolve all need to seek anything beyond what we are, because in that sweet surrendering moment of true acceptance we become witness to the totality of how divinely made we are.

If you take nothing from this transcript from my heart to yours, take this. Let it arrive at the heart of your being and rest there often, especially on the days where being human gets hard, because it is, but it does not mean you are doing it wrong or getting life wrong.

Soul whisper ~ Remember this

"You are worthy. You are loved."

Use this mantra below daily and often. It quite literally saved me from a life of perpetual self-loathing which had become my norm.

"I am love. I feel love. I see love. I am loved."

A soul gift – a way to use this mantra in a morning or evening blessing. Or even with another.

- Have some anointing oil – (grapeseed oil with some of your favourite essential oils – I love rose, frankincense, sandalwood and Ylang Ylang.
- Place some on your left hand
- Use your right hand to receive some oil
- Begin to anoint your body at the crown whilst repeating the mantra- "I am enough, I am worthy, I am loved."
- Continue through to the third eye, throat, heart, belly (womb/hara), root – (bottom of the spine) both feet and hands.
- Repeat the above mantra at every point with sacred oil in your hand.

This is a very simple yet deeply profound devotional act of self-love and care.

When I witness women offer this blessing to one another, our whole world shifts in ways that is understood without words ever being spoken.

I bring this blessing to my children, and they extend it to me in return.

It is a rich source of connection in my life.

Chapter Nine
Shadow Dancing
In The Dark

I am and always have been comfortable in the dark. I had at one point an addiction to my own terror; it was a comfortable old skin I knew so well. This shadow of inner terror followed me everywhere I went with a fixed belief that in the heart of pain was where I would feel the most gain. I loved being brought to this place as it meant I felt alive, felt something; it was better than numb.

It took time to recognise that it was not only feeling this part of me that was calling me home, but it was also freedom. This led to me discovering something softer as the years went by. Every time I gifted these parts of myself that liked to linger about in terror, a seat at my inner table- a way into my heart. Something opened, and a new way of being began to birth.

Each new year, there was a softening, a desire to reach for the light, and to be the light. To call more joy home and return the codes of innocence to their original essence. I would hear the soul whisper. The clarion call from my own soul lineage. To remember I was so much more than pain.

A soul whisper ~ Remember this

"Lighter my child, tread lightly upon this Earthly realm. You cannot fumble around in the dark forever. Remember who you are."

I met within me the challenge I faced with lightness, joy, laughter, and ease. I noticed that I clung to the dark where less of me was seen. To meet the light and be seen in it as the light almost felt too hard. Unfamiliar. Too unsafe.

I would ponder- how does one safely reach into and express joy in their body without another snuffing it out before it had its moment to shine? I did not know how. I just knew I wanted it, needed it, craved it.

This lighter life. More ease in my body. In my life. I let my soul whispers lead me to teachers, mentors, and friendships which reflected what this looked and felt like.

In my shadow dancing, I met the parts of me prematurely fixated on becoming the light before integrating its gift. Before integrating and seeing myself fully as I am. I tried to hold it too tightly in the beginning. The light. I tried to be in its presence only. I tried to make it the holy and only answer.

The only true way. I was supported by my spirit team to yes, go to the light and reminded it will be not necessarily be easier there until you understand the gifts of your darker moments. I can feel the contradiction of what I am bringing here. I could feel the questions of, "Well, where do we go? To the light? To the shadow?"

I have come to an understanding that feels right for me; it may for you too. This is that, as a soul and human, we get to hold them both, to dance with them both fully so that they may both come into the heart of our being- neither being right nor wrong.

Both need to be claimed, owned and fully alive within us. Accepted. Loved. Honoured for the gifts. The light opens us into more ease whilst simultaneously bringing us closer to the edges of our shadows, which is seeking more lightness in the form of love. If we stay too close to the shadows and deny the light and its presence to show us the gifts within those places, we miss so much about what seeks to be met in this body and in this life.

I recognise neither are to be shunned nor denied. Neither are to be glorified or pedestaled as the right and only true way. I get it can feel too much of an ask, given what we humans live and what we know we are capable of.

Who would ever believe it?

That those of us who know the dark so intimately could also hold the light so truthfully. That both are sacredly interconnected. That those focused upon the light offer a way to shine brighter, fuller, more radiantly, beyond what makes us fearful of being fully seen as we are.

There are those of us who are afraid of the dance, for who will join us there? Who do we become? Who do we leave behind?

What if we are left there in the light of our holy darkness even more alone than ever before?

Yet, I promise you this, if you dare to move into this dance, within the fabric of your entire beingness you will discover something so potent and alive that it awakens and stirs all your senses in this world and beyond it.

Everything is brighter. Everything is softer. Everything radiates with a beauty that words do not do justice to. Alone is not something you feel as you sense that you are connected to all that is within and around you in ways that nourish you from the inside out. This dance between the shadow and light of our soul is a continuous invitation into more compassion.

Chapter Ten

Compassion

To be compassionate means we can meet ourselves and others with a tender heartedness, a softness, empathy, understanding and warmth.

It is my belief that we can only meet another to the capacity we can meet ourselves.

It took me sometime to cultivate compassion for myself and this world we live in, for those that did not live up to what I needed in my life, to meet our world from a place of understanding rather than blame and fear.

I grew up believing I did not want children as I could not bear the thought of bringing life into this world at that time. I was very vocal about my desire to not be a mother.

Little did I know that motherhood would be the beginning of that journey home to more compassion for all of life, including my own parents and family life.

As I began to navigate the hurts from my past in a more compassionate way, I began to soften my gaze upon myself and those who loved me along the way.

This is a message that moved through me from Mother Mary as I began to meet the loving presence of more compassion in my life. Remember Mother Mary lived a human life, she was as human as you and me- a mother, a daughter, a sister and a woman of soul medicine ahead of her time.

Mother Mary Speaks

"It is so difficult to meet ourselves and others with a compassionate sincere heart when we are so entangled in the moments and stories of pain, anger, fear, blame and power struggles. It takes courage to meet all the pain, rage blame and struggle, to not fear it or run from it."

It takes skilled holding. I could not have met so much of my own had I not had skilled holding and a supportive sisterhood.

When we do find ways that feel soul safe, human safe, and soul nourishing, a beautiful feeling arises in our ability to meet life- past, future, and present- with a certain grace and humility. Granted, it takes a huge amount of self-responsibility and self-awareness to allow the grace of love to move through us fully. Know love is always present and is always flowing.

We are simply not always knowing of its presence or of the gift that tries to move through us, through all of life.

Compassion for ourselves and the lives we have led is a most difficult state to reach into when we have had difficult life paths to lead and, honestly, also have very much attached ourselves to the stories within the mind. Where the wounds of our heart lives.

Where we fear abandonment, rejection, ridicule, and betrayal.

Dissolving attachments to that which we make define us can help, allowing ourselves to take a breather inward and drop ever deeper into the heart's wisdom that we can never truly be punished, excluded, left out, or even left behind. We can then rest into trusting ourselves, using our own discernment about the directions we wish to take in life. We are no longer afraid of being misunderstood. We soul flow in the directions that feel most heart-aligned for us as individuals, connecting to likeminded and hearted divine humans along the way.

When we come home to this understanding, we begin to see that each of us plays our souls part in this human life. That we each have a purposeful gift for the other. For the world itself.

We would recognise the endings as openings along our life path. See the closed doors as beginnings. Extending grace to those who do not get to walk all the way through with us, nor us with them.

Often our humanness clings to what is familiar, not seeing the gift in the mystery yet to unfold. With every opportunity to drop deeper into soul wisdom, her vision. The sacred Mothers prayer for the Earth and her children.

Even if the direction of that call is now different to what we envisioned, it is still a collective call. Even if we do not all walk in the same direction all the time.

Our purpose and destination, I believe, is still the same- which is to open, awaken, remember, and seal in the highest vibration of love's call where possible.

Our heart and soul whispers are all the same.

To love and be loved in return.

I do not believe this changes, no matter how often we incarnate.

We all hear the whispers and calls back to love in any given moment. Back to hope, back to freedom, back to acceptance, back to compassion, and back to us.

I have felt this call like a pulse within my womb, which in truth is deeply connected to the womb of creation, where a gold thread of love and recognition is fully present.

That ache we sometimes feel for mother is not always our birth mothers of this lifetime. It is a deep gnosis that lives within us all, all genders, all beings that know we have a golden thread of connection to the cosmic womb of all creation.

That know intuitively, even if we cannot say what it is we know, that we have been ripped apart from what truly matters.

This is never not true.

When these threads of holy connection intertwine amongst all of life and the ways we experience relationships, the opening connections, and in the dissolving moments when relationships shift, this cosmic thread of life that sustains us all simply begins weaving another pattern upon the tapestry we all know as life upon this Earth.

Every time I drop into this gnosis and vision of our deep connection to the sacred mother, I can only ever feel compassion mixed with grief, and a humbling acceptance for the ways life plays out in our awkward human ways.

Our divine tasks are always still flowing and growing.

Our human minds often still hindering and opposing.

We are often told the key is to silence the mind to hear the heart. I am of the belief as I write this, that befriending the mind is a kinder way in and through. Befriending the mind helps us soften into the heart so we can hear its whispers beyond the confusion of the mind.

How do we befriend the mind?

Did you know the mind has up to 3300 thousand thoughts per hour? I didn't until I looked it up and this is what the experts have discovered in their scientific research.

So, how do we know …

- Which thoughts to believe?
- Which are our own?
- Which are imagined?

Truth is, from my perspective we don't. However, that doesn't mean we are powerless against the thousands of thoughts that run through our mind.

We do have opportunity to explore the thoughts we manage to catch along the way.

We do have opportunity to consciously work with our mind and our thoughts.

How?

- Stay curious about your thoughts
- Ask, is this true?
- Do I really believe this?
- Is this real and is it mine?

As you play with your curiosity, you will develop skills naturally that clear out thoughts that pull you down into spirals of doubt, insecurities, and feelings of lack and unworthiness.

You become a gatekeeper of your own mind through staying curious about what thoughts land and make decisions about whether that thought gets to stay and play havoc with your wellbeing. This frees up our energetic field to be able to drop into the heart with more ease.

Obviously, this can be more complex with chronic PTSD, depression, anxiety and trauma responses to life. However, as someone who experienced all of this, I know this can be of genuine help and support as we learn to navigate our lives freer of what feels hard and heavy.

The answers we seek in this life can be found in connection to the heart. Grace lives there, and in grace we recognise we always have a new moment.

When I speak and share in live events, I am always reminding us about compassionately meeting ourselves, especially in these transitioning times when so much is being brought to us; much of which is yet to be fully understood.

Every in breath and out breath is a new moment and a new beginning. It is an invitation to grace if we struggled in a moment. It is a powerful reminder to honour the sacred pause in-between breaths. A soul sister once shared with me that in the pause in-between each breath is God, creation itself. Ever since this knowledge was brought my way, I have never breathed the same again.

I mean, what a powerful piece of knowledge right there! That in the pause, the in-between moments, lives creation itself.

What I took from that was that in the sacred pause, the breath in-between- the moment where all that there is- is stillness. There is a moment to allow creation itself to move through you and breathe the next moment into existence as you do.

This feels personally powerful and activating for me, I am hopeful it is for you too.

It is a new moment to choose, and to truly honour all parts walked singularly and collectively. In true grace, love compassion and humility. Where no blame is placed, judgement is paused, and shame gets to rest for a moment.

I have come to understand that we get to choose every single time and here is something that can help with that.

A reflective question to move into when compassion or acceptance for self or other has left the room:

- Reflection: "What would love do now?"

Then respond to life through that contemplation, where possible.

Try it for a day or two, a week or month, everyday use it as a devotional practice committed to love, especially amongst your most difficult connections and relational experiences.

Witness it soften your heart yet strengthen your ability to care for you and those around you in ways that honour all involved.

Chapter Eleven
The Art of
Letting Go

Please know I am a stubborn human. I do not let go of past hurts easily. I do not always know when it is time to let go. I have ordinary everyday living struggles in my life, relationships, and motherhood. There is a common question I am often asked, and I want to give it space to be answered more fully here for you.

"When doubt and insecurities arise in my life, what do I do?"

I hope that it gifts you something of value that you can take into your moments of doubt.

I was not always someone who could let go of much. I was the kind of person who would hold onto everything. Every hurt, odd or angry conversation, I would be ruminating for days, weeks, months, even years over stuff that would overtake my mind. I was all sorts of paranoid; insecure and doubtful that I was liked, never mind loved.

It impacted my self-esteem for years and my ability to allow loves breath into my being so it could rest there and fill me up in her presence. Over the years, things shifted. It was for me slow, steady, small steps towards a space on the inside where I could breathe easy.

There were and are still things that have helped along the way. I have mentioned a few already- energy work, womb wisdom and healing, ritual, and devotion to a path of remembrance and presence all helped.

I noticed and understood that these feelings of doubt, insecurity, feelings of lack, unworthiness, and fears of being ridiculed or, God forbid, misunderstood all played a significant role in learning to love myself more.

Each had a distinct purpose and gift for me to unwrap.

Note the ones I mention here are my personal gremlins or friends on the inside; it depends on the day. I invite you in this moment to insert the one that is most frequent for you.

What I noticed and understood was that they never truly leave, not really. At least this has been true for me.

They morph into something else, quieten down and can linger in the background like a quiet whisper. They are sometimes fully silent and met in peace, at other times one or many can arrive at the room with me for some attention.

In this moment, I have two choices- I can let them consume and direct the path ahead, or sit with them lovingly, inviting them to share with me what it is they need me to hear, feel, meet, and own. It's uncomfortable work, shadow work. I know I have touched ever so slightly on it; it is an important part and a piece of this journey you and I are on together in this life at this time in our world.

Another way I work with letting go is I drop into myself- my why, my vision for this life, and for this world, I remind myself of the vision that dropped into my heart in 2009. I reimagine my little self, starry-eyed looking out the window of my bunkbed, imagining a world full of safe homes for all of us.

I remind myself of all the lives I have touched by having the courage to meet what churns up inside of me and meet it with love, to share the journey with you.

When these friends or foes on the inside arise and I am struggling to let go, I often also drop into my heart and remind myself about what I do.

I author this book at silly times of the day and night when it's quiet. I have noisy children and I must make time for me to visit here so you can get the best of this journey I have invited you all along to. I must write at silly o'clock. Just before I sat down to write this section, doubt washed over me as a flippant comment from someone I loved threw me in a bit of a spin.

I began to heart link to myself a technique I learned in IET (copyright to Stevan Thayer). As I heart linked, I began to speak a prayer to the divine.

A heart link is creating a golden thread of connection and love between you and the Angels of IET, you open your heart and send love towards them, and they send it back to you tenfold. It's a very beautiful way to tap into the love that is available to us in any given moment.

I asked to be reminded why I do what I do, why I am authoring this story, and why I show up in life the way I do.

I could not sleep, and here I am writing about letting go and how we do it, unable to let go of something that was said to me just minutes ago! The irony of the ways in which my life has reflected the very things I am writing, to be sure I am doing it too. I love how this works.

I let go tonight when I dropped inside and remembered my why.

Examples of how I let go and let love in

- I re-read testimonials of every human that has gifted me one. I read these words and remember I played a small significant part in a shift someone made in their lives.
- I celebrate the moments- the ways we humans through our connections enrich one another's lives. I remember the moments.
- I recall your why. Even now, your moment of choosing to be here in these words is worth celebrating.
- I call upon that which is divine in my life and let it refuel me with renewed faith.
- I meet doubt with compassion, and I let her have a moment. I remind her it is safe to move out into the world and to let go of what holds me back.

- I re-ignite the fire in my belly that I was born with, and I trust in letting her in that I am creating spaciousness for something miraculous in life.

I invite you here in this moment to feel into the niggles, the doubts, the insecurities, fears, and anything that may be lingering. I invite you to imagine for a moment you are throwing it in a fire pit.

Imagine you are there dancing your way through the flames and moving out towards the world in ways that feel soul aligned and true for you.

Then read this…

"I meet you in the dance in-between.

That place you arrive where no one answer is fully clear.

That destination where there is a fork in the road

Hesitation Which path to choose.

What to let go of?

What to hold unto?

This is a moment amongst moments that has our head in one place, heart in the other

It asks you to lean deeper into trust

It asks that you move without knowing fully where you will arrive

It asks that you dance with the mystery of life and love.

You feel the distractions

Pulling you this way and that

It almost feels deliberate.

A confused humanity is so easily controlled

So many versions of reality existing in one place

So many possibilities to live out loud at any given moment

Right now, you are here with me

I am inviting you in to contemplate

"What is truly important in this moment?"

"Who truly matters to me in this life?"

What I decide need make no sense to anyone but me

I follow my own golden thread of trust In doing so, I strengthen trust in myself.

In my life.

I trust in what falls away

I trust in what stays

I see what I am devoted to

I see the simplicity of choosing myself in this moment

I see ease become the way

I am devoted to those I love

I am devoted to living this life in ways that feel aligned and true for me.

I am devoted to spending time on what truly matters to me

I am devoted to discovering what truly makes me happy in this life.

I am open to being inspired

I am creating more laughter and joy

I invest in myself in ways that feel nourishing and fulfilling

I ask for support when needed

In my devotion, the forks on the road that fill me with doubt seem less daunting

I let go, I let in, I let be

I feel safe to do so

I rest into the safety I am feeling right now I rest into trusting myself

I trust what breaks me open is supposed to

I know I can gather the shards of what feels broken and uncertain, and put together a mosaic of possibilities

I feel and see what is asking to be let go of as doorways into the heart of what needs my loving attention and care

I offer this kindness to myself right now with my hand on my heart and say thank you for opening my inner gifts of

Courage

Wisdom

Hope

Faith

Compassion

Freedom

Truth

And mostly for bringing me back home to love.

Love is what we are."

In this moment, I wish to share that I am in awe of us humans in our ability to love and let go, let in, and let be. To meet ourselves in love repeatedly even against the perils of human existence. We always find our way back to love.

When we are grieving in Ireland in particular, we know how to love in grief. The way we wake our beloveds, the way we hold space for the tears, loss, and celebration of life at the end is a gift so few of us take time to acknowledge.

Even when our lives are falling apart. Even when the ones we thought we were here to love forever become the ones we need to let go of. Love is still there breathing life into the aches of despair being felt. When we are lost, broken, afraid, uncertain, angry, or frustrated, we still meet and be in the presence of love.

We still feel it pulsing through our veins. We still know it when it arrives at our worlds, even if it is felt like it has been a while.

We all still believe that it exists.

That it is real.

That love is part of us and, in knowing this, the letting go parts of our existences become a little less daunting and more necessary. In doing so, we create more space for love's breath to fill us up with her presence.

We learn the art of letting go and meet the power of acceptance in our lives for all that is and has been.

Chapter Twelve
The Gift of
Acceptance

I want to move into the power of acceptance in our lives. One of the biggest shifts I had to make on the inside to keep showing up as I was, was to move beyond my fear of being misunderstood, ridiculed, and labeled insane. I have had very painful past life memories surface over the years around this inner wounding and very painful present life experiences also.

I recall a moment of clear reclamation and the words that flowed out into the public. I am sharing them here. I believe they will comfort those who feel the judgements strongly as they are opening. It is my hope they will soothe any doubts or fears as you feel increasingly of what cannot be explained by logic.

I began a very public post on the sacred world wide web with the following words…

"Let's talk crazy."

"Let us examine all my crazy.

Right here, right now.

It has been thrown my way plenty and often.

Right here, right now I am taking the fear in my mind of being seen and known as crazy head on. I am allowing you to witness my crazy and what it has gifted me…

I get why people would believe it to be true. I understand why I would fear my mind sometimes of that label and being so sorely misunderstood. I mean I publicly speak aloud that I commune and talk daily with God/Goddess, Christ, Mother Mary, Mary Magdalene, Angels, beings of light, and spirit guides that are unseen.

I mean, some would say it's no different to man walking into a chapel to pray to a GOD they fear, yet I promise you it is met with much more scrutiny than manmade religions.

This part of my existence in this ordinary extraordinary life I live asks that I paint these beings. That I share their words of wisdom for those ready to receive them. I speak into how they guide me, deeply protect me, love me and gift me experiences that are otherworldly, in ways I often cannot explain as these moments of my every day must be felt to be known.

Sometimes my experiences are like the greatest acid trip you could ever imagine, only I have not taken any mind-altering drugs. Of course, to those looking in who have never experienced beyond the veil of our humanness, what I meet in my life looks and sounds crazy.

Right? Yet I know I am not alone in this experience. I know there are millions of souls right now experiencing magic beyond the veils of our often-limited perception."

It is true some of you reading this book will begin opening to this. It is possible that many of you with this book in your hands are already here with me.

I think of that saying, "Those who danced were considered insane by those who couldn't hear the music" ~ George Carlin.

My reflection on examining what is crazy continues…

"Of course, so much of what I share sounds and looks crazy to those who do not know or experience the world as I or you do. Who do not see as I see. Yet this is my life, and the truth of its experience, of what moves me, makes little to no sense. You may find your own life taking a similar turn. That you find a thread of golden wisdom compelling you to speak, seek, and find in ways that are unusual, yet it will become usual for us all as time moves on.

It is just some of us got the clarion call sooner than others. Our hearts were broken open differently to hold a certain frequency as we shift the masses out of our sleep slumber. I want to offer comfort and share what my crazy has brought me.

In my crazy, I began to let go and release myself from everything that was feeding my other crazy. The part of me who could not, would not, and simply did not know how to be happy in life.

This crazy invited me every day into more acceptance, contentment, and happiness. We can all be a little more than allergic to claiming what is ours.

My crazy guided me to find passion, love, laughter, joy, and compassion in all of life. Even those parts we find hard to hold, meet, and love deep. I was remembering the gift of nature, the nature of my being, the power of prayer, the holiness of life and our very existence. I would dance with sacred touch, breath, and heart-holding opening to a spaciousness that was guiding me further into my own embodiment.

I was remembering what it was to be alive and recognising increasingly the miracle we are. Simply because we are. Understanding the innocence within that was seeking expression. It returned me fully into my body here on Earth after I had been shattered into a million pieces because of a series of events that no child should ever have to live through.

It is activated within my heart a drive that leads me daily into the knowing that we are seeding in a new Earth grid of love, hope and safety for all of life. This crazy so many of us fear, misunderstand and judge gifts us respite through our most challenging times. It has brought me to my knees more than once to witness and hold myself in pain where no one else could or would be able to.

It has gifted me a brave heart that no longer fears those places my other crazy was running from. That other crazy was addicted to escapism, drama, and numbing out through misguided experience and connection.

Opening to what was otherworldly inspired me to paint again, to create from my heart, to share these paintings, and begin to make a living from my passions. From this space, I reclaimed a confidence in my writing an began to share these words with you. Finally, after so many years, some of these words have made it into the pages of this book that you now hold in your hands.

I finally found the courage to share more of myself. To hold and share what I perceived as faults, strengths, and my raw humanness, including all the fears that ran through my bones, often very publicly, just like right now.

I have profound respect for those of us who go first, who show up, unedited, as they are, as we are. It gifts us all a moment of realness to meet so much of ourselves, minus the shackles of shame we all carry that weigh us down. The more I met what was seen and unseen inside of me, the more inspired I was to collaborate with you all. Something inside of me spoke and understood how to hold many.

A wisdom revealed itself beneath the pain of my life and the story lived out. Gratitude replaced resentments. These wonderous moments and experiences opened doorways of possibilities and returned me home full time to nurture and be with my children.

In this lifetime it feels important that I am the one present there. I was meeting continuously an exquisite love on the inside that was stirring awake so much of what was stagnant, unmet, and unloved.

This crazy part of my existence took me into the heart of depression. It took me to my ugly, right through to my inner self-destruction buttons, which I had genuine habitual attraction to detonating several times a week at one point in my life.

The hardest parts were meeting the ways in which I had harmed and inflicted pain upon others. Not so I could hurt more, only so I could love more. My crazy showed me how beautiful I am, how beautiful we all are. I use the word beautiful a lot in my life, in my world. I do not feel we tell each other enough just how beautiful we all are. We humans hold and move through immense challenges in this life and still we love, that is the most beautiful thing in the world to me, that we can exist in this love, even if life brought horrors beyond words to live through."

The art of acceptance is not easy. Take this book for example. I am almost 43 years old. I have written and rewritten this book several times and deleted it after. I first started to write it in 2016!

This time I moved into the acceptance that if I am to get these words into your gorgeous hands, I would need help. I accepted and made the decision to collaborate with a mentor, Katie Oman, not so much because I struggle to write, but more for accountability in seeing it through to publishing.

Acceptance is a hard one for so many of us. We divine humans often struggle to accept ourselves. I get it, I truly do. What I have come to believe is that we are all a little bit broken, a little raw from living and loving. Often unsure, doubtful, and twisted out of shape. Some of us more than others.

In lovingly accepting this as a soul truth, it helps us navigate this world with more compassion for ourselves and those around us. Life throws a lot our way. Often what comes our way offers us opportunity to gain experience.

Sometimes the lens through which we are choosing to look at life is clouded, and it can be more than difficult to see life with a fresh new perspective.

None of us are perfect, I often ask, "Is that the point here in this life? To be perfect?"

I do not believe that is the aim of life; certainly not for me. I have a desire for simplicity in my life. To live, explore, play, and become the best that I can in any given moment for myself and those I love.

For me, it is enough. I have no grand desire for a big life, only a life with plenty of laughter, experiences, and good company. Thus far I am blessed. You want to meet my children; they are the best company! Highly entertaining and continuously funny.

Contentment arises from acceptance. From letting go of any grand plans and simply dropping into living from the heart.

When I move through life from the still point within my heart space, everything shifts from being hard. Something shifts from the inside out and I see it reflected to me in ways that take my breath away. It fills me with gratitude. Acceptance brings us right into the energy of gratitude, and a grateful heart is a happy heart. In accepting myself and my life as it is, I live more courageously, in each moment as it is.

Many of us fail miserably at being true to ourselves when it matters, many times over- myself included. Yet, the more I moved into the art of acceptance, the less I lived for others approval, and the more freedom I felt to flow towards the direction my life path was guiding me into.

How can you drop into more loving acceptance?

- Validate yourself
- Create and honour your boundaries
- Keep your promises to yourself and others
- Connect with those who you know will celebrate you when it matters
- Release those who harbour resentments towards you and your life choices

- Choose your own path fearlessly often and plenty – it gets easier the more you do it
- Spend time in nature, in the quietude of your own heart and ask the right questions about the direction of your life path
- Choose yourself
- Say no more often
- Say yes more often

Examples of this include leaving teaching to paint and share my own art; choosing to relocate because my heart led me even when everything wasn't in place; and choosing to take my younger children out of school and home-educate them rather than stay within a system I know is wrong for their life path.

Calls to living our truth are always rooted first in our own discomfort. Especially if it goes against the grain of what is familiar and societally acceptable. Yet, the joy of this life is that we get many invitations into living it more fully each single day. So many of us are caught up in what we think is living, that we miss the invite to be alive, fully alive in our truths, in our beings, and in our soul paths.

Every breath is a new moment. Every invitation in life is call to more love, more compassion, and more acceptance. It's okay to have growing pains, to meet our discomforts, and to fall into the egoic traps of fear and inner dialogues of "what ifs?". We all meet doubt. We all must dig deep for courage at times. We all struggle to own and express our truths for a myriad of very valid reasons.

Life happens to be a twisted tail of experiences, all of which root us back into the heart in one way or another. I ask you- what if we began to celebrate our greatness rather than our smallness? What if we honoured our holy inner truths and lived by them more fully every day? What if we said no when we meant it, and yes when we wanted it?

What if we could get beyond the stories of entanglement into our sovereign selves?

What do I mean by our sovereign selves?

Sovereignty in this moment of our evolution for me is to recognise the power that lives in us. To choose our life path beyond the false hierarchal systems that exist in our world. To be sovereign is to be connected to the source of our own power, connected to the source of creator (God/dess) and to act from this knowing. To not be chained to false laws of governance whose motive is to control, harm and interfere with our evolutionary journey.

A soul whisper ~ Remember this

"When we each recognise and remember our part in this great love story, humanity and our world will know peace."

What if we created spaces and places where there was so much safety and love that it was made easy for us to drop into acceptance for all the places we hurt, raged, and lived in regret?

That we gave space to allow ourselves to open new pathways of loving and living, each seeing that we all carry a personal weight in this human life, and no one is any different in that.

I personally have yet to meet another human that has not been hurt or hurt another.

I have yet to meet a human that does not desire to be deeply loved and met as they are.

For us as a collective and as individuals to heal the hurts lived out on this planet, we must first accept that we have each been harmed and have harmed. Both as perpetrator and victim.

Imagine with me for a moment.

- We have gathered all of humanity in one room

- We have invited all to close their eyes
- To take a moment to feel the sensation of their breath
- To take a sacred pause
- Then we invite them to open their eyes
- To take a sacred glance at the human in front of us.
- To witness the whole human in that sacred gaze

We would meet the same longings, pain, discomfort, and more in that space.

The invitation here is to support those around you in more love, to call into being acceptance for yourself, to ask daily on the inside…

A soul question I often hold close to my heart to guide my path is "How can I best serve in life for the highest good of all today?"

Soul gift: Examples of how love and acceptance support us in this life.

Love …

- Is not always soft
- Is sometimes a firm no against certain patterns, behaviours, relationships, and experiences, both on a personal and collective level.
- Opens doorways for us to walk through into finding ways to move beyond these things.

Acceptance …

- Does not deny where healing must happen, or where wrongs must be made right.
- Invites us into witnessing what is in front of us with enough compassion to make sound decision for our lives.
- Brings us closer to the world we all long for on the inside.
- Gifts us the courage to love more, deeper, more freely, and more truthfully.

Soul whisper ~ Remember this

"Acceptance is the call to more love- for us, our world, and those we cross paths with."

To accept all of who we are and what we bring to this life is to move beyond our blind-sighted despair of life that we feel is happening to us. To allow ourselves to move to a space of I have a choice: a choice to love and accept where I am in this life. A choice in how I let myself be supported in that, or a choice to continue my spiral of self-loathing and self-destruct.

I know this life offers us many a choice point at different crossroads; I have met them. I now choosing something different is not always the easiest choice. Sometimes I have chosen wisely and others I have chosen the harder path ahead.

None of these choices were wrong necessarily, yet the impact of choice was and is felt regardless. In choosing to love ourselves, we choose to recognise when we need extra buffering, holding, and support.

It is vital in this life we have people who can deeply hold, guide, and help us navigate so much of what arises for us in this life. Without this level of safety and love, we are like a raft out in an ocean storm, alone and drowning in pain. We do not need to go this life alone. Yes, there are times when a solo walk matters and is as equally valid and yet, when we are moving through our own murky waters on the inside, it matters who you have on the outside.

For so many of us this will not be our immediate families. Not because of the absence of love, but often because it is simply too close to home when healing and accepting life as it was, and, or is.

It will often be people we stumble into in life. Dear soul friends and sisters, mentors, psychotherapists we trust, and holistic practitioners- if you are like me that is. My point being to choose wisely. In my life

I have sisters I go to for my blind-sightedness; the things I refuse to see about myself that prevent me from moving onwards.

I have sisters who build me up and remind me what I am made of when I forget. I have my encouragers, who are fun-loving and help me to let my hair down. I have honest, true, and loving supportive beings around me. I have chosen wisely, and my life is full because of this choosing.

The art of acceptance is about understanding that in this life we come to learn, unlearn, and relearn. In doing so, we often grow, and expand. We learn to let go when it's truly needed as I will share more later when it is not, and in doing so we meet grace only hold what is needed. Through acceptance, we learn grace and come to understand and see clearer. Often, we begin to discover love has a way of overriding everything, even in the bleakest of moments, if we have the eyes to see that is.

Chapter Thirteen
Grace is Home

What is the meaning of grace?

> Dictionary meaning… "eloquent, smooth transition, generosity, kindness"

How does one move through life with more graciousness, kindness for oneself and each other?

On this path of remembering, we are often taught and called upon to cleanse and clear ourselves of negative feelings, emotions, and experiences. It is good practice to clear and cleanse our physical, emotional, and mental energy bodies. However, I have personally struggled with this so many times as it began to feel like a rejection of the most valuable teachers on the inside.

Getting curious about these teachers often opened something different.

My curiosity about what it might feel like to begin a dialogue with my shame, anger, fear, guilt and all the parts in between that I had been trying to clear myself from softened my approach to healing. I stopped rejecting these vital messengers. I stopped believing they were any less worthy of my love, time, and attention. I stopped trying to pull them out from inside of me. I stopped ignoring them. I did this and was ready for this work after working with energy for a time. IET helped me find the courage to go deeper.

It is so easy for us to love the parts of ourselves that are more readily accepted in our world. The real work is learning to love and accept ourselves and get curious around why we fear others will abandon us, as well as why we abandon ourselves.

The real work is making peace with and sitting with the rage, anger, fear, guilt, and shame, and seeing that each hold a gift and are present for a reason. I noticed and paid attention to when I got angry, for example. I discovered quickly that it was usually from a space on the inside that was not feeling safe, that felt the need to protect me or those I loved.

What unfolded had a certain beauty to it. Leading me back into more acceptance and compassion. These two are playing a huge part in the story of this book as it reveals more of itself to me, for you.

In gifting myself full permission to be with and love all that I was and all that was being felt- for I am all of it and all of it has a place in my life- a messenger to something that was pulling at my heart for attention became clearer.

I was better able to discern what was mine and what was not. I was able to hold what was mine and find better ways to express it rather than have it spill outwardly into my life in ways that were harmful and destructive towards myself or those in my care. Where am I now with it? I am still in "it" and still inviting it all inwards.

A soul tip for navigating the hard stuff.

- Don't assume a person can hold your pain
- Ask them "Do you have space for me right now? I am moving through something hard."
- Don't assume everyone has the skill set to help you navigate your complexities as you shift your life path. Learn to know the difference. Seek professional support when needed.
- Have people around you that are privy to your blind spots and sensitivities. They will be the lifesavers and transformers in your life

This work can be navigated solo if we still are listening, still opening dialogue and understanding, within the context of safety with our wellness as a priority. It took me years of intense work both professionally and personally to be present to what scares me about me. Wisdom is hard won when we try to do everything ourselves!

I have discovered over the years that if we are overly focused on clearing out and feel no further ease within ourselves that it can be a doorway into trying something different.

What to do if what you are doing is not working for you?

- Being present to what is being felt is important
- Be honest with yourself about what is not working
- Get curious about why it is not working
- Be sure to validate, listen and respond to what is being felt
- Move beyond denial into the truth of what is being revealed to you

For years I gave away my personal power. I gave away my mind to self-doubt. I gave away my dreams to fears. I gave away my love to hurt. I gave away my body to those who did not deserve her. I gave away my peace to anger. I gave away my authenticity to falsehood. I gave away so much of myself that I began to really believe all the lies within my small mindedness.

Whilst all along the discomfort, pain and feelings were messengers and guides. Each were in active service by reflecting to me all the ways I was trying to escape myself. The grace landed when I began to treat myself and all that lived in me with kindness. Changes happened when I trusted what I was experiencing and let my intuition guide me to the right mentors and support.

Until this point, the martyr was having her way; the victim was wallowing in self-pity and blame; and the fear was thriving strong. There was no escape.

I was not of right mind. I was of the mindset that I needed to clear myself of being a victim, of being angry, of raging, of my shame. The truth was and is still that I was a victim of horrific abuses.

There is a teaching in spirituality that says "there are no victims in this world" I personally find that blanket statement insensitive at its best and downright dangerous at its worst. There is no shame in speaking to and honouring that part of me or you, more fully.

I seek to give her space to breathe and be validated and acknowledged.

Of course, I was angry. I was not protected. Yet, I felt the strong need to protect the feelings of those around me more than allow myself to meet what was true in me. The soul truth I came home to rest in my heart is this…

- No one in their right mind torments themselves so.
- The mind of separation would, but no one connected to the truth of source would.
- No one connected to love would. God. The one of many names. Nothing and everything. Think about that for a moment.

Grace lives were Goddess lives. In our hearts.

Love would not shame or blame us for feeling what is needed or necessary.

We can lovingly close certain chapters in our lives that were difficult. For so many years of my life I chose the mind of separation. I was learning, growing, and being initiated into being even before I entered the womb of my mother for this life. Life pulls us in so many directions and veils of separation are placed upon us through the ages.

They separate us from our cosmic mother, our higher consciousness, our truth and wisdom, love, and from source. These veils of separation are thick and strong. They keep our hearts apart. They create longing we do not always fully understand.

Soul tip – remember this

- Love would never believe anything less of itself.
- Love would never believe itself unworthy or not enough.
- Love would never believe itself less than any other being.

Often life leaves our self-esteem in tatters, and it feels tormenting, emotionally and mentally.

We sometimes recreate scenarios in our life that reinforce our feelings of lack and unworthiness. The challenge on a soul level is to remember who we are at our core. We rehash the same triggers, old woundings, various places, spaces, people, and the same repeated cycle until one of us shifts the sails of our generational ship towards a new destination.

It is like the girl who grew up with an alcoholic, abusive father and she dates or even marries one- just as her mother did and her grandmother before her did. Until someone says no, leaves and decides to choose differently.

My only prayer for a husband when I was a young girl was that he didn't have smelly feet or drink excessively. How easily pleased my young maiden was!? I married such a man, admittedly in my own humorous way I joke now if I had known my prayer would be answered so fully, I would have made a bigger list of what I wanted!

Many come from families who had little to no emotional regulation. Big feelings were chaotic and met with a lot of drama. So, someone decides to spend their life mastering their emotions, leaning into them rather than away from them. So, it becomes about having compassion for past experiences and enough grace for yourself as you try it differently.

For me, speaking up and out about sexual abuse in our family, put an end to that secrecy and shame, ensuring that we as a family guide our children into knowing and understanding their own autonomy and right to be safe.

For example, with my own children I do not teach them that every elder automatically deserves respect. I guide them into understanding. Respect is a two-way relationship and is one they get to be part of and make decisions about. Including with me and their father/s.

It is important for me that my children know they can say no. They can choose not to participate in any experience that feels off to them, even if it is saying no to something simply because they don't feel like it.

It is important to me that their feelings are met, seen, and validated. Even if the adults around them do not value this, they know I do.

A child who feels validated, seen, and met will come to less harm to a child that is not seen, heard, or met. These subtle shifts, or not so subtle, are often soul calls from our higher consciousness to more love for ourselves. We often stumble clumsily at times through life and the wheel turns slowly for us. But it is turning. We are shifting in collective and personal awareness as a humanity.

Some of the ways I feel and see the shift in our collective.

- We are making different choices.
- We are paying attention to the world around us.
- We are walking many different paths.
- We are asking questions
- We are learning to lean into our tired, our exhaustion, and our big feelings with far more empathy than before.
- We are recognising that it is less about blame, and more about presence to what is true for us.

I like to believe that we are all moving towards the same direction: a more peaceful world and life for us all. It is like we are all hearing whispers in the wind.

Sometimes, on a soul level, it feels like we are big toddlers inside adult bodies, learning how to navigate our world in a gentler way for all of life. We have been planting flowers, watering them, and they are beginning to bloom worldwide. Something both new and ancient is arriving day by day.

It is such a soul exciting time to be alive. It is a tough time too, no doubt. My own heart fills with hope daily. What I was talking about and moving into 20 years ago, a decade ago, a few years ago is being felt right now on our planet. This is huge. I feel a love affair of the greatest story being born where we merge human and divine as we recognise increasingly the truth of our origins.

- We are past the blame game into curiosity about why we do what we do.
- We are using our triggers as activators into lives worth living.
- We are becoming enthusiastic about creation itself and asking big questions.
- We are loving our hurts rather than harshly judging them.
- We are beginning to see how worthy we are.
- We are taking up space.
- We are giving ourselves full permission to dream into being a world like the one our hearts remember and long for.
- We are taking small steady steps towards the very things that light us up and get us excited about being human.
- We are looking each other in the eye and asking for more-respect, care, love, and understanding; this is basic human care.
- We are taking our power back a little at a time. It is not always easy. It was never going to be. Life simply is not easy.

Our sacred intentions are different. Our ability to meet ourselves more fully are softer. We are truer to ourselves. Grace invites us into our truth, into loving our darker moments- our lies, our fears, our sadness, grief, anger, and rage- so that we may return to the innocence that lives within us and the knowing that we have not ever been forsaken.

We are and will always be loved, held, seen, and met. On the hard days when we feel most alone in it, the messengers will come and ask:

Can you be here with me, as I am, and love me now, love you still?

This is the power of grace beloved friends. For your heart is immaculate and pristine, lighting the way for you in every moment.

I ask you take this and write it somewhere where you will find it easily on the hard days. Speak it aloud whilst looking in a mirror when needed.

"Know you are worthy of love. Especially now when you are struggling to believe you can be loved. I love you. I am with you. I value you. I respect you. I hear you. I am here for you."

When to let go of letting go…

Often, we hear from well-meaning people after something hard happens, "Let it go." Or, after a disagreement, "Let it go." Yet we often struggle to do just that. Grace doesn't force us to "Let it go." It softens us into accepting what is so that we can finally feel peace descend into what is or was hard.

It's bloody challenging work this letting go business and at times insensitive of us to demand that another does so. It is a journey, it is something that takes time, depending on what or whom we are letting go of. At times it's messy and brings us through a myriad of experiences before we can breathe easy and finally feel free, if ever.

I recall the time of the court case, it was complete. I was dropped off at my friend's 18th birthday celebration. It was the 5th of March 1997.

The man who sexually abused me finally admitted guilt and was sentenced to jail. It was over. Right? I mean, every other person just kept saying to me that it is over now, it is time to let it go. Only, I was looking at them and nodding my head in agreement saying, "Yes, I will, I will let it go." But, on the inside, I was terrified. I thought there was something wrong with me because I could not "Let it go." I could not let the pain go.

Truth is, for me at least and many more of you I know because I have worked with enough humans this past 13 years to know, that often we are not able to "let it go", which is why I speak into compassion, acceptance, and grace so often. So, this is an invitation to let go of the idea that you must "let it go" to live a fulfilling, satisfying, and contented life and find peace.

Now, this is not saying we should stay wallowing in the pain. It is about making peace with who we are at our core. I have shared how pain for me was a comfortable old skin I knew well. This shadow of inner terror followed me everywhere I went. The terror I had come comfortable with softened over the years and invited me to live differently. To choose differently for myself, my health, wellbeing, and for my own sanity. I breathed peace into those parts I had spent my life raging against.

My path did not become about only letting go; it became about letting in. Letting in more of who I was rather than who I was not. I suggest we stop fretting and getting caught up on what we must be, and instead recognise our light within the dark for the gift that it is. It is then I believe we do begin to shine more brightly, a beautiful love unto and into the heart of ourselves, one another, and this planet.

I discovered that in letting the light come into the whole of my being to fill me, it became important for me to recognise that not all of us, not all of me, would make it through the gates of life's traumas fully healed, unaffected, or fully whole like I once believed.

It will feel important for you to know this too, so you can finally breathe easy and let go of the idea there is something wrong with you if you cannot fully let go.

You see, on the beginning of my path of remembrance, all my focus and expectations within this work throughout this healing journey was to fix myself and make it all better. I wanted to have it all replaced by a shinier, glossier, more perfected, and acceptable version of whatever the "new" me would be. I was missing one of the biggest pieces of this lifelong puzzle we live in. I was not seeing that I could be loved and accepted just as I was. That I am and always have been enough. I hope you take this one message into your life and remember all your days that…

"You are enough. Just as you. Loved just as you are. There is nothing you need to do to be loved."

The deeper I went on this journey, the clearer it became that it was always about recognising my own worthiness and understanding that it has always been about loving what is present right now.

I ask you, can you Love all of it.

All of me.

All of you.

All of us.

For we are it all.

I have come to letting in the belief that there will always be a small part on the inside that will bleed lifelong. That this is okay.

That this is not something to fix or even be sad about, or to feel I have failed somehow. In fully honouring this and seeing this for what it is, I understood that this small mighty part of me on the inside is so very brave to be willing to carry the whole of me that is unable to move beyond pain.

That is a gift. I may not have always known that this small mighty part of me is willing to hold and be with it all so that I can live more fully, in love, in joy, and in lightness. I do now, and how I love her so. Knowing that it is okay for this small part of us to have a moment to feel and be as it is. To know that this part on the inside is the most perfect, beautiful, whole part to being human after all. Is something to cherish and hold ever so gently in your loving hands as a sacred truth.

Chapter Fourteen
Presence

Presence Speaks …

"Let me take you by the hand and hold it for a while in mine. Let me gift you the presence of my heart as you courageously stay present to what is moving you right now. Let me guide you to trust in yourself again. Let me show you a way in and through. Let me see you and show you it is safe to be seen."

How does one come home to presence in a world full of distractions?

We come home to presence by identifying what the actual distractions are.

In our world today it is so easy for us to become distracted. I am laughing right now at how easily I became distracted just as I was about to write into being present. How did I distract myself from being present here to the writing? I jumped on Facebook to announce my word count. Whilst there, I began scrolling and lost myself in a moment until I caught myself again. It is so easy to be distracted.

Examples of distractions:

- The stories we tell ourselves.
- The modern days news

Which is enough to turn anyone's head in a spin. I believe it to be a classic tool of distraction away from our internal intuitive antennae about what is true and not.

Not everyone agrees and that is the joy of this varied life. However, for me, I stopped watching and engaging in the soap operas, the TV dramas, the news drama, the fame dramas. It became part of my own spiritual hygiene, and you are welcome to try it too.

What is "spiritual hygiene"?

Ok so let us consider this for some understanding. You have a physical body, every day you take time to nurture your body. To bathe it, clean it, choose what you will adorn it with, what you feed it, how you will move it, rest it and be in your body. Imagine your energy field and all that it absorbs daily.

Imagine it accumulates over time, as this energy builds up, layer upon layer upon layer.

It begins to feel clouded, hazy, unclear, and you become aware of this. In this moment you have choices to make, and you will make these decisions according to how you feel energetically.

How can I support my spiritual hygiene?

Pay attention to…

- What you watch
- Who you listen to
- What you listen to
- What you read
- Who you spend your time with

Ask yourself regularly if what you are spending your energy and time on is adding to you feeling energised or not. If it is not, it is time to make some decisions about this and to make some changes.

How will my energy be impacted if I do not make choices to support my spiritual hygiene?

Some examples of how this may impact you are:

You will feel …

- Tired
- Drained
- Exhausted
- Uninspired

- Confused
- Indecisive

Why do I feel the need to be mindful of what I read, watch, and listen to?

I believe it pulls us out from our lives into the lives of another, or something else that honestly, from my own felt experience, drains our life force. We get pulled in and distracted by habitual patterns- one example is gossiping. I am of the belief that choosing to engage in gossip is a way to avoid tending to our own gardens. Many humans, including myself once upon a time, find it difficult to weed out their own internal/external gardens and choose to distract themselves with another across the road. I get it, it is easier, yet it is less fulfilling and takes us away from our own power and ability to lead our own lives.

Other examples of distraction is our inner saboteurs- the parts of us that fear our success in life, and which feel safe playing it small. If you can grasp clearly what a distraction is, you can meet it.

Soul whisper: - Remember this

Distraction feeds off our insecurities.

Think of women and the number of businesses that distract us from really owning our innate beauty by playing on our insecurities, feeding our doubt, comparison gremlins, and envious tendencies. It takes courage, fortitude, and self-discipline in a world agenda that thrives on us believing we are less than to be present to how much more we truly are, and how much more we can bring to life in this world when present to our sacred soul gifts.

So, back to the question: How do we be more present?

"We become more present by first becoming aware that we are not."

Just like I shared in the beginning of this chapter about myself becoming aware of my need to distract when I was needing to be present. We can become aware of our inner dialogue; it helps us become present to what is going on for us on the inside. How? We listen. When we learn the art of deep listening, we become more present.

Soul gift – A practice for deeper listening

I spent a whole year one time listening to my need on the inside to respond with something rather than truly hear what the person was saying to me. I was not always aware I jumped in, interrupted, or didn't let someone finish. This practice was inspired by the desire for more presence in my life.

How to implement this practice.

- Listen more than you speak
- Really pay attention to what is being said to you
- Repeat back what is being said to you – it helps people feel heard and understood
- Use statements like "I hear …"
- Notice how many times you want to speak before someone is finished.
- Practice the sacred pause before you speak
- Repeat – rinse – Repeat

I sometimes must return to this practice even now as my mouth often opens before I think. It is a devotional practice for sure!

Once the awareness lands, the invitation to be more present and listen will too.

For me, this practice felt like I was rewiring my response to life and to people so I could be more present. This, of course, has been immensely helpful in my work and mentoring of women. If you are not sure how distracted you are or how present you are, try this over the course of the next week or so, to see how deeply present you are to hearing those around you.

It will feel like a vow of silence for a while- no responding back until people have been fully heard. It is not something we humans naturally have and often needs refined through presence. To answer the question that I asked in the beginning of this chapter more fully:

How does one become more present? We become more present through deep listening, which ignites a new level of awareness, trust and safety which in turn opens new ways of being.

There are very real distractions that eat at our own self-worth and stop us from believing in our own power. There are very real agendas on our planet that bank on us never being able to push past these distractions. They can be very clever in their manipulation and may look like they are good for us- fun even- even though they are detrimental to our health and wellbeing.

We are living at a time on Earth where many of these illusions are being shattered. We are seeing so much for what it is. Seeing beyond the stories we are fed as normal. Truths are being revealed daily for those with the eyes to see and ears to hear. Less and less of us are shrinking and more of us are rising, even if we are shaking. We are in the dance of in-between. That place we arrive at where no answer or path is fully clear. There is a fork in the road and hesitation on what road to choose. One of distraction, or one of presence.

We get to choose in every breath. In every moment, we get to choose. None are right nor wrong. I feel momentum building upon our planet where a moment of all moments will arrive. Where we will be asked to drop out of the mind into the heart, into the body, to let it lead us beyond what feels logical or even makes sense. It will ask of us to trust and lean deeper into community with one another. We will have to make decisions quickly in the moment, not fully knowing if we have made the right choice or even into what we have fully entered.

These moments will arrive fast and thick, and collectively we will all be and have been invited to choose the way of presence- presence to love, connection, community, and each other. To allow ourselves to move beyond I into us.

The mystery of life will become ever more present. And still the distractions will come pulling us this way and that. Deliberately so, for a confused humanity is an easily controlled humanity.

Right now, there are so many versions of reality existing in one place. There are so many possibilities to live out loud in any given moment. To stay present beyond distraction asks so much from us. These can be helpful reflections that may ground you in presence...

- What in this moment is truly important?
- Where is my heart right now?
- Who in my life truly matters right now?
- Where is this moment leading me?
- Why is this important to me?

When we get present with our own inner dialogue and beliefs, we can discover so much of what we felt, and see what was not even our own, and so we can begin the journey of unravelling the knots within. Rather than me explain how to do this, I am including a short effective Mary Magdalene meditation practice on a way to be with this.

A soul gift - Unravelling the knots within meditation

- Gather a piece of cord

- Feel into 3 knots of tension in your life right now
- Knot each into the cord
- Call upon the energy of Mary Magdalene
- Begin to unravel, untie the knots and feel them dissolve energetically
- As you untie the knots and feel them unravel begin to feel into what you would like to have in its place
- Redo the knots this time calling upon the energy you are desiring
- Wrap this cord around your wrist as a gentle reminder of what you are calling into your life

As we unravel within what is not true for us through presence, we may start to make decisions that make little to no sense to those around us. This is okay; stay present to what is true for you in those moments. Others are not walking in your shoes or living your life.

Presence invites us into a new level of devotion in our lives. I love the word devotion; it is a word that makes all of life sacred. I often contemplate what am I truly devoted to in my life right now. This helps me get present to what is important and what is not. You too may find it helpful.

When we are truly devoted to a path, a way of being, or a life choice, the forks on the road do not feel so big or daunting. The parts of us that are lacking in trust settle into the parts that are leading in love. It is my hope that as these words land in your heart, that they land softly and open a deeper level of trust in yourself.

Examples of what presence is for me

Presence for me

- Is never having to deny how I truly feel, or hide who I am.
- It is not pretending to feel a certain way or force a connection that is simply not there.

- It is not worrying about support and being able to take up space, and a reminder of my worthiness in this life.
- It is safety in love and knowing I am loved.
- It is knowing I am deserving of support and compassion for the times I feel differently than that.
- It is being able to find the calm in the eye of the storm, as well as recognising I am in a storm and not the storm itself.
- It is about cultivating safety in my body after years of being numb to her.
- It is practical in its love and devoted in its gift to us.
- It is understanding, empathic and holds the ability to advocate for oneself or those in need.
- It is to be aware of yourself and beyond yourself.
- It is the ability to quiet the mind and access the heart
- It is about learning to trust in oneself again after not knowing how to for so long.
- It is about being curious with the tender-hearted part of ourselves.
- It is dancing with grief and joy all at once.

Presence asks we be with the fullness of what lives inside of us and outside of us. It asks that we rest into it and feel its softness. It meets the parts you reject and reacquaints them with your friend's compassion and acceptance. Imagine if presence were a human, she would speak softly into the heart of our beings…

"I am here for you now and always; I always have been, I always will be. Bring me all of your exhaustion, dear child of mine. Your soul is tired- human tired, heart tired,

emotionally tired, mentally tired, spiritually tired, and

physically tired. I know you are not in need of fixing or repair, just a soft landing to rest for a while."

Imagine- our beautiful body temples would relax and tears would gently wash over our cheeks. No sound, no drama, no pity, no wiping away of those long-needed tears. There would be no judgement, only full presence. We would not stop. I have had and created moments just like this in full presence.

Where there was no push to shift the moment. Where the tears gave no reason for their presence but were simply felt and met. We humans change in moments like this. I have witnessed it often in myself and others. When we are met with full presence with no one trying to fix us, we often take a deeper breath. It feels strange at first to us, and then we exhale at the level of safety being offered in the moment.

This is the gift of true presence. We release the pent-up feeling, our contracted state becomes relaxed, and we soften our armour. We simply cannot hold this level of presence for another unless we have been modelled it or offered it towards ourselves.

Presence will show us time again that we can be tired and inspired, sad and hopeful, fearful and excited, hurting and expansive. Presence invites us into ownership of both ends of the spectrum into simply being where we are, with what we are, and whom we are with.

In recognising what gifts presence bring, we make peace with the distractions and sometimes even welcome them. I can too acknowledge that not all distractions are there to harm us. There are perfectly wonderful ways to be on this Earth, doing things we love to do. Just stay present and all will be well.

What are the gifts of being present? Honestly, there are so many. I touched on that already, yet there is more and two aspects that were particularly potent for me in my life. Presence brought me home to my body and to the joy of being more fully present in my relationships.

The beauty of being present within my body was a completely new thing for me. I spent so much of my life punishing my body, running from her, letting her be used, denying her a say in anything really, going against her nature, and so much more.

At one point in my life, I struggled to look at myself. I was convinced through my own vision that my face was slanted and disformed. It was strange for me when I started to see my true reflection. I simply was not seeing myself at all. I would see pictures and not recognise myself.

I had not heard of body dysmorphia until later years in my life. However, on reflection, so much of what I felt and experienced within this body was just that.

My relationship to and with my body was directly linked to the impact of my childhood abuse. For many years of my life, I was in a body yet rarely present in her. It became very clear to me, as I began to move through this path of remembrance, that I could not fully arrive at love until I gifted myself the full presence of being in a body. I began to wonder about ascension, about the ways we all too easily want to fly high into what we assume are higher realms of existence. I was at this point very able to easily journey where I felt in both the dream time and waking time through meditative practices that I had become familiar with.

I could also see how easy it was for me to want to ascend beyond my body, even when every fibre of my being kept calling me back home into the body. It almost felt like an eternal fight, even though it was internal and felt very much like it was mine alone. I could see on a much larger way how this has been the battle of the ages, the most ancient one, the one that has been fought and lost for a millennial, repeatedly.

Still, we choose to return. Still, we choose to be here with her, our beloved Gaia. In this space, beyond all time at the same choice point, we continuously meet as souls, as humans, as star beings on a planet with all and everything. Still, we do not see, still we forget, still we fight, pillage, destroy and deny the gift of our bodies and what it means to see, feel, and experience life as vibrantly as we do here on Earth.

As I write, I am recalling a moment I was walking, and my gaze was drawn upwards into the skies above. It was a beautiful blue-sky day, sometimes a rarity here in Ireland. We have beautiful skies all the time, just rare that it's sunshine blue.

I say this laughing and smiling, with tears rolling down my cheeks as I sit here writing these words for you in the company of two soul sisters. We meet once per month to share space and keep each other accountable as we grow our sacred soul passions and businesses.

I am reminded in this moment what a gift it is to be here right now. I am facing a window and the sky is now also vibrantly blue. The sunlight keeps catching my screen, making it difficult to read what I am writing. So, I soul flow into trust that what I am writing is of value for you all.

Back to my blue-sky day where my gaze was drawn upwards. I could see an opening in the sky, as if the heavens were reaching down for me to notice. I could feel and see so much in this one moment that felt like an eternity. Yet, in human time, I am sure no more than a few minutes passed. In this time, I remembered my first time on Earth. I remembered my choosing to fall from the heavens unto the Earth. At first it was curiosity of my soul that brought me to this sacred planet.

As light beings we have no idea of what it is to feel, smell, touch, or taste. The density on our planet is both gift and curse.

We get to decide which it is.

In this sacred moment where I am drawn towards the sky, all those years ago and often in present day moments, I am reminded why I am here, why I keep choosing to return, and why I will choose to continuously return.

To arrive here on Earth often feels like a curse, yet it is a powerful gift to be here. To experience the polarity of our existence, both light and dark. To know love, fear, and joy.

To have a body that can be touched, met, loved, and gift us the most exquisite experiences. To feel the pulse of a heartbeat, to feel the blood run through our veins, to feel the softness of our skin, the breath itself.

Discovering how to breathe and how to work with and use my breath and be present in my body has been one of life's greatest gifts. To feeding my babies from my own breast, to growing my babies in my womb, to birth my babies through my vulva- I am in awe of our bodies and what they can do.

I am of the belief that the human body is creator's greatest creation; it is the most powerful technology on the planet. It can self-heal most if not all disease; we have simply forgotten and become so disconnected from what exists within us.

On the small end of the scale, look what happens when we cut our body temples: she heals. Within moments, a scab will appear and begin to work on our behalf to heal the wound.

We women bleed every month and do not die. She releases what she needs to from our wombs to keep us at optimal health. I am of the belief that our bodies are a continuous loving messenger to how we are truly doing in this life and how much we love ourselves.

We chronically abuse them and still they serve us miraculously, working harder and harder to clear out anything that creates harm within us; we call this disease. I say it is dis-ease within us- years of harmful foods, nonmovement, alien substances- and still she serves us, beautifully.

In our world we need intermediate help now to heal because we have lost ancient wisdom, which in my heart is a direct reflection to how disconnected we are to the Earth itself! To the feminine. To the ancient knowledge that pours through, seeking connection with us.

My body, our bodies, are a sacred ancient creation that hold soul keys to so much more than any of us experience in our lives.

We are starting to remember and to be more present. There are aspects of soul remembrances being activated worldwide right now and I feel the ancient mother calling her children home to being fully present in mind, body, and soul. A most sacred trinity within.

Presence goes way beyond us. It invites us to explore the way we are within our relationships. I would have said I was very present in my relationships as a friend, daughter, and sister, yet truth be known.

I was barely present with myself, never mind having the capacity to be present with other humans.

My children were the exception, and it is because of them that my ability to relate and stay present shifted. I mean, have you ever tried to ignore a child that really wants what they want? Children by their very nature demand full presence and they will become your mighty sages in calling you home repeatedly, if or when you try to drift.

Chapter Fifteen
Stepping into
Power

I always say you know how present one is to feeling joy when you watch them with a child. My first born, for example, demanded I care for my body. To stop smoking, drinking, and eating foods that made me want to vomit, for the time she was in my body. She demanded that I feel everything- every tear, every fear, every moment of doubt I had about myself, and this was all whilst she was in my womb.

When she was born, she flooded my entire system with the presence of love that I had not ever felt nor known; it almost felt too much. I was beaming with love at this beautiful being who, bless her, chose me as her mother. I never ever felt quite worthy of my children for years- of the love, the presence, the endless opportunities to play and be playful, and the ways in which they compelled and pushed me with no words only presence to be a better human being.

I often look at them still. Now there is six divine humans who chose me to be their human for a moment in time as they grow and stretch into their own life paths. I think of a piece of writing inspired by a conversation with my now 5year-old. Feel the power of her presence in these words.

"She tells me she is a rainbow wolf with white hair with magical powers to crack open the earth. That today the Earth will crack open even more. I believe her! This morning she declared today was a wonderful day as we are alive and can feel everything. She uses the word wonderful a lot. She tells me I am not her real mother that here on this planet I get to be her mother. Like an aunty. I try not to take it personally. She tells me that she chose me because I have the universe in my belly. She rubs her belly and shares about the universe in her belly. She calls on me to slow down as she whispers to the flowers saying the fairies have gifts for her.

She dances for and with the trees. Taps them, talks to them, and sits with them. She tells me what they say to her. She doesn't like her hood up as she likes to feel mother's rain on her head, as she calls it. She sings happy morning every morning. She says I love you a lot.

She kisses my belly every single day and tells me I am so beautiful. She smells me and tells me I smell like roses. It is very clear to me that she overflows with a love for herself and her being here on this planet. Naturally grateful. Naturally attuned to the elements. Naturally able to hear and see what is hidden. Naturally connected to love that she is. Naturally embodied. My job as her mammy, I mean guardian aunty, is not to mess up the magic that she lives with. We adults often think we know better. I don't know about you. I wouldn't mind being a rainbow wolf that can crack open the world for a day or two."

I am often more than not in awe of them. Sure, I meet frustration, overwhelm and have often burned-out being mammy and holding all that means. I struggled with their calls to presence to begin with. My eldest son had a thing for bringing me right into all the places on the inside I still struggled with, often in front of large crowds.

I mean what a gift! Being seen, being heard, being met! He would be there, loudly proclaiming what he wanted/needed at barely two, and there I was, an almost grown woman. I was still incredibly young, in my early twenties, and not able to speak to or ask for what I wanted.

I would observe my children and, what others perceived as "bad behaviours", I often instead chose to see this as invitations to become more present to needs being met. I was far from perfect in my younger mother years, and even still, yet I tried, I really tried to be all and more for those little humans that chose a young woman still trying to find her feet on this Earth.

I am forever grateful that they chose me and redirected my life path, for without those two little humans this story you now read would have been quite different, and I am not so sure it would have ended well. Presence brings us into power, personal power- the power to shift and change our lives towards destinations that feel more soul aligned.

Holding our own power in a world that has often abused its power is hard. Even hearing the word 'power' can bring up lots of feelings, and they are not all good feelings. We often feel powerlessness in this life, in this world. Powerless in what happens to us as children and even, yes, as adults too. Yet, we rarely lose sight of the power of love, and what is possible when this power rests upon the right hands. We all know this and have felt it.

Love is a constant alive on this planet and inside of people, no matter what the world shows us. Love is real, it is here, it lives in you, me, and us. This is what holds my unshakable faith in the heart of humanity, though others may call it naivety. I am not so naïve that I will not challenge abuse of power when I see it. So many of us are born with this compulsion to challenge what we know and feel is wrong. This compulsion is soul led. It is what makes so many of us become activists on this planet.

Activists of peace, change and environmental causes that truly matter. This shows up in a myriad of separate ways, helping shift the axis of this planet towards its intended direction. Women's work is the work of a true warrior and activist on this planet right now. Revolutionary in its nature as it activates and reminds them of their inherent worth and value beyond servitude. I always had this energy within me that would stand up for the underdog. A memory of standing strong against a bully at the tender age of 11 years old comes to mind as I write.

I could not stand to watch her treat another so badly and found myself standing up, even though I was shaking, to say no more. I have met more moments in my life- true calls into my power. No more to hiding the lies and shame of a paedophile at 15 years old. No more to men that did not care for me. No more to work that felt soul destroying. No more to patterns of harm that were cycling through my everyday living. Often, we are handed the keys of love to use it for the power of good.

I feel the feminine rising like this in our world right now. Standing up, eye-to-eye, to that which is creating harm, yet still underestimating her ability to access great power to create profound change.

We so often underestimate ourselves and are often sorely underestimated by those who feel the power is all in their hands. We live in a world as mighty and gorgeous as it is, whilst having certain energetic programs in place to disempower the masses. To have us believe that we are powerless and unable to bring change into our personal and collective experiences.

This could not be further from the truth. We are power beyond anything we have ever imagined. Just feel back into an experience where you had to dig deep, stand up, and make a change. You may have shaken, you may have swayed to and fro, yet you did it. YOU DID IT!

Just as I have many times. We often fear owning how powerful we are, for we have been taught to fear ourselves. So many abuses of power have taken place, and right there with that abuse of power lives a benevolent power that is constant and never-ending. It is limitless in its energy and capacity to hold and redirect us back on path. When we start to come home to the power we hold in our own hands, we will also meet all the ways we have harmed and not used it wisely.

There has never been a more important time than right now to drop into all the ways we abuse power in our hands. We need to do the work required to ensure when it fully lands and opens in us that we do use it for the power of good, for all.

I often sit and imagine from within my heart space a vision of humanity, firmly rooted in the seat of our power and knowing exactly what is being asked of us. In this moment, I would love to invite you to take a moment and imagine what a humanity rooted safely into our power with our hearts wide open and receptive would look like.

Imagine them using all this power for the good of all and directing that energy to where it is needed most to bring harmony, balance, and ease into the lives of us all.

Soul gift ~ A Meditation to support our collective

- Close your eyes
- Feel the sensation of your in breath and out breath
- Imagine a rose within your heart and its beginning to open
- This rose is pink
- The energy is compassion
- Fill yourself up with this compassion
- Feel it fill every part of your being ~ physically, emotionally, mentally, and spiritually
- Take all that you need and then, with the excess compassion, begin to imagine it is being sent out from your heart
- First to your family and loved ones
- Then to your community
- Then to those hurting in most need
- Then to those in lead roles on our planet
- Imagine then we are all gathered around the globe
- Holding hands
- Hearts open
- Filled with the energy of love and compassion
- Feel this energy expand towards everyone there
- Feel the vibration of love being shared between you all
- Every human, all sentient life is being filled with this energy
- This love is pouring towards all of life, every blade of grass, river, lake, molecule of water- infusing the entirety of our planet
- Imagining a world filled with the energy of compassion and love

- Sit with that in your heart space
- Feel gratitude for this experience
- Let it fill you
- Let it remind you of the power that lives in you
- Let it fill your days
- Let it influence how you move through your days
- Journal on your experience

Imagine if we all did this one soul practice daily morning and night. Imagine the change it would bring into your life and those around you if you were vibrating with this energy throughout your days.

I have been sitting in circle with women for 13 years and within those circles, with women from all over the world, both online and in person, incredible things happen. I know the power of collective prayer.

Have you ever been in a room full of open-hearted women all praying aloud for the world and its children? It would make you weep, both in joy and grief. For it is joy and grief that calls us together. When I am in circle with women, I am not interested in a fantastical version of who she thinks she ought to be. I am there asking her to meet herself in the fullness of her own power. I want to feel every woman's own unique soul voice, her heart song, for in that moment the entire world feels her arrive more fully than before and we change, our world changes.

For this is the truest channel of change any woman can bring to life and reach into. Within her bones lives cosmic stardust, whispered into her being to call into remembrance, at the perfect and right moment for us all.

This is her direct link to the source of love and power that birthed her and carved out every inch of her being into existence. I have no doubt in my mind, heart, body, and soul that it is the true voice, essence, and spirit of the feminine as she rises to reclaim that which has been suppressed. This world needs this right now! I see us eye to eye, womb to womb, and heart to heart- standing together against all that has raped and pillaged life on this Earth, from ourselves to our children, to the Earth.

I believe with the whole of my being that when women the world over come in touch with the source within her, she will reach a state of soul truth that will be an unstoppable force of miraculous change for us all. It is happening, I feel it strengthening each day.

Only yesterday I was walking to a soul sister's home whilst listening to Spotify, and the song Ancient Mother came on. Instantly, tears fell, and my womb opened and connected to the cosmic womb of the Earth. I saw a visual of the women rising, holding, connecting, and coming alive. More alive than they have ever been. More ready than they have ever been to say no to what no longer can be on this Earth.

I felt us strong, protected, and together. My heart felt like a river flowing in all directions into the Earth's rivers and I kept seeing faces of women I know from every corner of the Earth. I felt a silent bow of gratitude extend from my heart to theirs and from theirs to mine.

This is the power that is returning to us, to us all, and for us all. In moments like this, I feel most alive and know that we are truly in this together, even if at times we feel so alone in it. If you can for a moment take some time, right now, to listen to your own soul whisperings, it will fill you up with not only your own power and soul song, but also as a sacred reminder that you are not alone. It will remind you that walking with you are legions of others, both in this world and beyond, supporting you on your return to innocence. Remember this when you begin to fear your own rise in power and voice on this planet.

It makes sense that we sometimes fear our own power rise in us. We have many a memory, both in this life and past lives, of being punished, shamed, excommunicated, disowned, and even killed. For daring to stand in our truth, using our voice for good, and being powerfully aligned with our gifts, passions, beauty, bodies, sensuality, sexuality, and the Earth herself.

There is a powerful quote that moved me quite some time ago. It spoke into how it was not witches that were burned, it was women. It often was not men throwing us into the fire either- it was other women, afraid for their own lives and the lives of their children. So, we turned on each other. We remember this in our bodies and not always our minds.

Many of us are born with an innate distrust of the feminine and never know why, until we begin to dive into this path of soul remembrance and discover the roots of our witch wounds. Witches were, and are, you and me. They were women who understand the way of the land, who danced with the wisdom of the moon, worked with womb wisdom, herbs, the Earth's wisdom, and elements.

Women who know what it is to hear and work with the whispers of the wind, the music of their souls and the eros within. We were once upon a time freely sensual, alive, wise, revered, embodied and highly psychic.

With a real understanding of the art of ritual, how it impacts shifts, and energetically creates something powerful and purposeful. Those of us who know this wisdom, understand the power of every word spoken and recognise it as a living prayer, an invocation, part of a ritual, an experience that alters our reality.

In our world, many rituals take place in broad daylight, unconcealed and manipulated in ways that deceive us into consenting. For the law of the ancients is known and consent is always required.

With this now in mind, we can become aware of the power we have to consent or not to the words spoken and the spells being cast upon us.

The deceptions take place cleverly behind the veils cloaked as good for us, necessary even. We do not need to be aware that we are part of a ritual. We give it consent by joining in with the words, the actions, and the momentum of whatever is taking us in. It is necessary in modern times to understand the power and intent behind what we are participating in. Our world is awash with energetic practices that are not all fully understood, nor do I claim to have full knowledge. What I would say is that discernment comes with experience and practice, be it in this lifetime or over many.

I would offer that before you extend or offer anything of your energy, that you find solid soul-led mentors. That you learn how to check inwards, and that you take the journeys inwards that may not always be pleasant to take. If you do not, you will never truly know if it is a wounded part of you working through an entity attachment or if it is your heart leading the way.

What is an entity attachment? "An entity attachment is parasitic in its nature, an energy that manipulates you, your thoughts, and emotions. It can be a soul who has lost their way that was attracted to your light, a misled soul energy that feels it is offering you protection, a past life connection, a soul part that was severely traumatised, or a repressed part of your own darkness/shadow that has yet to find peace within. Many people fear entity attachments yet in its truest form it is simply energy, and this energy can be met, loved, and dissolved so it no longer has any power over you."

How do we know if there is an entity attachment in our energy field? "It is not always easy to know if we have an entity attachment and not all energy practitioners can work with this energy. As sometimes there are similarities between what is dis-ease in the body and attachments. Some are very manipulative in their energy and feel like love when coming into your energy field. Discernment and regular spiritual practice and hygiene are important. We may have an entity attachment if chronically fatigued, in pain, feeling disorientated, constantly anxious, depressed, struggling with addictions, in environments that are constantly chaotic, feeling like we are being watched, of having unusual sensations within the body. Which also can all be easily explained by other rational factors. It's best not to jump to any fearful conclusions and if you are feeling off or unsure. Seek out a seasoned energy practitioner who knows what they are doing and ask them to help you see what you might not be able to."

Can I clear an energy attachment myself?

"I would say mostly yes, unless it's a particularly dark manipulative energy that is tricky to work with. What I do know is this, that nothing can live in or on you without your sovereign consent. So, declaring that out loud with a statement like "I ask anything that has been uninvited by me to clear from my physical, emotional, mental, spiritual and sexual energy field to leave now. You are not welcome here." is a most helpful and powerful practice to clear your field of anything that has arrived uninvited by you."

Have I met this in my own field and/other in working with others?

"Yes, to both in myself and others. In myself, it was tricky. I felt like a crawling up my spine- like something was trying to open it and climb into my energetic field. Along with it came a feeling of intense fear and a knowing in my heart that what was moving in me energetically was not welcomed. It helped me strengthen my discernment about what and whom I allowed into my energetic field, life, and presence. With another, one example I will give- I was working on a woman and saw first within my mind's eye an attachment to her solar plexus (stomach area – power centre). As I saw it, I then felt what its energy was like in her field, I felt the tremors of anxiety that she carried with her, and I saw when her energy became weakened through alcohol and how it entered. I was able to guide this energy towards the light, as it has attached to her light and only wanted to be in the presence of love. This changed how I viewed entities and helped me understand that not all meant harm, yet still do cause harm, as they lower our energy, vibration and pull us towards feelings of dis-ease within our lives."

I recall a time I was being made aware of what an entity felt and looked like within others. I directly asked the question to be shown. At first, I was shown how they feed off our addictions- particularly alcohol, drugs, and sex. I was shown how some people become dead in the eyes through the addiction. I could see the entities looking at me through a person's eyes, and it was quite difficult to observe this in real time. I often contemplate how different we would deal with addicts if we recognised sooner that it is not the actual human who is addicted. That it can also be an entity attachment spiraling them deeper into the pattern of addiction as it feeds off their life force.

All of this is an invitation to become aware of what you are consenting too, why you are, what its intent is, and if your heart feels it or if it is ego led.

I am gifting my perspective from my own experiences, and they may or may not resonate or meet you right now. I trust that, in my honest sharing, it is meeting those needing to hear it. One of my constant prayers throughout my own path of remembrance is to be shown if or where something not of love is working through me. I work with a lot of people, through immense life challenges at times- their grief, pain, traumas, fears, losses, gains, celebrations, and soul remembrances.

This constant prayer to serve cleanly from a place of love has led me into the depths of my own unworthiness, narcissistic tendencies, co-dependent patterns, entity attachments, selfishness, addictive nature, greed, fears, and insecurities.

Anything on the inside that was disempowering me and feeding energies that were not safe for those collaborating with me, or unaligned with my higher heart purpose, was presented for clearing. This led to what many call a repeated dark night of the soul.

What is a dark night of the soul?

"A dark night of the soul is a way to describe a moment of initiation that can and does feel dark in its nature, as it often brings with it pain and despair. It can be activated through a traumatic life event or through our own willingness to meet that which lives in us. To know thyself. It is something that lasts much longer than one night and can spiral us deep into the depths of our own being for many weeks, months, or some years. Put simply, it is when we make a transition from one state of being into another. It is when false egoic layers release and we meet the light within us so that we may walk lighter and wiser upon this Earth. I personally feel collectively that we are all in this right now to varied degrees. Those who have walked through their own soul work are holding the light for the collective right now."

7 signs you may be experiencing a dark night of the soul.

- You are feeling disconnected from your life and what once interested you.
- You are feeling a sense of isolation and are not quite sure where you belong.
- You are feeling a lack of motivation and a strong desire to rest more.
- You feel bone tired and heavy in your heart.
- You are asking "big life" questions, pondering your life, its direction and purpose.
- You are experiencing and sensing something beyond this world.
- You are exploring what it is you truly want in life, beyond what you have been told you "should" want.

A path of power, of soul remembrance, our birth right to return to innocence, asks a lot from us. Which is why we need solid mentors, soul sisters, and honest human beings around us.

Find teachers who walk in and through their own lives with a fine-tooth comb, ensuring that what they arrive to you with is authentic, honest, real, and embodied. whilst gifting them the grace to be human; not forgetting they will falter.

Remembering they are not responsible for the pedestals we may choose to put them on. No more than they are for our disappointment when they fall from it.

There is a lure with power that can feel tantalising. It offers us false promises, and along the way we will be invited into seeing the world as it is.

To become witness to the systematic programs at play that inter-fear with our ability to hold our own sovereignty, we must understand the dance between what is true and what is false in our lives and world.

For me, this is unfolding naturally through my life. I could always feel and know when I was in the space of someone or something that did not hold the light of truth.

Part of it was my hyper-awareness, due to the trauma of my childhood. Part of it is due to the way I am soulfully made.

It is often that from incredibly early in our lives we have well-meaning people around us, denying us the right to express and be with what we know and feel to be true. Often, due to their own inability to be with what is true for them. So, we stifle one another in a bid to protect and nurture, not recognising the harm being done.

How do we break through the matrix of our world? The systems in place that are made look like they are there to support us? When the only thing they support us in is our lives of work, eat, sleep, and rare moments of play.

We are born into lives where most of us are then placed within a school system to nurture and educate. I am not sure about you, but I know a rare human that fondly recalls their formative years in education. This is through no fault of the teachers, more the systems in place. I have, over the years, grown strong opinions about schooling, education, and the choices we make that we think are right. Most of them make people uncomfortable as it means questioning what they have known as normal; the right thing to do in life.

I have my children again to thank for the shift in my world thinking. I had some who were struggling massively in this system of support for their education.

One left the school one day at seven years of age. She walked out and put quite a compelling argument as to why she didn't need to be in the classroom to learn that life was about learning.

I remember looking at my little girl, baffled and overwhelmed, and thinking I cannot possibly educate you! How? So far, we have come from believing in ourselves that we the parents choose often to believe our children's care is best at the hands of governmental systems, and strangers. Rather than seeing that it's better in the hubs of their homes as they explore life! Only, I was not ready for this shift then. I had two small babes at home, two almost teens, and there she was asking me with sound judgement and making valid points to let her leave school at seven years old.

I resisted and, to her and our detriment, she became increasingly miserable. I began to ask myself: what am I doing to my child? Like all soul breakthroughs, they often begin with us questioning an area of our lives. This was one of those breakthroughs, the breaking through the matrix moments in our lives.

Fast forward a few years, and we have created a life where our littlest children are now all home. We have created jobs free from binds that restrict our lives, movements, and ability to choose where we place our time, energy, and honestly so much more.

This is, of course, one example. There are so many I could have given, yet I share to show that a path of remembrance will ask important things of us, brave things, things that go against the grain of what society and even our families see as normal.

It may ask you, like me, to become very vocal about life, to step up and out to be more visible on your healing path home to yourself.

We breakthrough systems that are not aligned with us at timelines that I believe are destined for us as individuals. Yes, it's true many in the collective could shift on the same timeline and many make the moves together.

Do I believe that those who choose differently are less powerful or soul aligned than I? Absolutely not!

We are all on our destination paths and all play our role in this life in this world. Each one of us reflects something of the collective matrix back into the whole. What we choose to do with what is brought to us is personal, and yes, I keep saying it as I believe it to be true, very much a collective momentum towards great change.

Soul gift

Some ways to breakthrough and make a soul shift

- Honour your soul calls (a soul call is that thing that gnaws at you to make a change)
- Pay attention to and stay curious about what is uncomfortable for you
- Be honest about who and what you are
- Find trustworthy people to share your path with
- Choose to believe we can and will do better as individuals and as a whole

The more we do this, the more we root into what is our true power, and the more enlivened we feel to be active in the direction we wish to see this world go in.

Do we have a destined outcome already paved out? "I am not so sure right now. All is possible right now and so many paths are open for us to walk down."

Will we all choose the path of the heart, to awaken and remember what is possible for us? "I do not know. I want to believe, yes, that enough of us have chosen the path of the heart, and it is felt known and will be reflected to us after the tsunami of discomfort we are choosing to walk through right now."

So much of what our modern world is built upon will collapse and must. Those of us holding onto the reigns of the past will struggle with this the most.

We will see so many of the most powerfully led industries be challenged increasingly as our world falls into the right alignment with Universal law. We will see so many masks fall and what we have celebrated and glorified crumble. Including those we wear ourselves. Honestly, beloveds, you could not have chosen a braver time to walk this Earthly life. You were born for these times and, even if you struggle to grasp what is happening from a day-to-day basis, know that there is a hand of love holding steady what rocks us to our core.

Ways you can support our collective personally right now.

- Take ownership of our own inner and outer worlds.
- Get honest about the ways we move through our lives.
- Begin asking daily in each moment- is love moving in me right now?
- Pay attention to what we consume and why

- Face the ways we are unkind to ourselves and each other.
- Look at the ways we are unkind to the Earth herself.
- Become aware of how we love and relate in our daily lives. (Is it love really in the driving seat? Or fear?)
- Pay attention to the way we treat our most vulnerable.
- Become conscious of how we treat our body temples.
- Pay attention to how we treat ourselves, the feminine, and the mothers of our world.
- Seek to listen more to the children of the world.
- Seek to know the truth and to live more truthfully.
- Learn the art of conscious communication.

How we treat ourselves, the feminine, the mothers of our world, our children, and the wildlife is a direct reflection to how we treat the Earth, our home, our heaven on Earth.

Our Garden of Eden is here, not out there, or up there. It is alive in you, it is in every blade of grass, every butterfly, every ocean wave, sunset, and wind whisper. It is here, waiting for you to connect to its vibrancy, its vitality, and its aliveness.

We cannot do that when we ourselves are numb to the life force that lives in us! When we come home to the heart of this one truth that we are all interconnected, we will arrive home to the heart of our purpose in this life. A purpose that binds us all, that keeps hope alive when we are in despair. This is what calls us all into action when it truly matters, a purpose that is driven by something we cannot see or touch, yet all know is there.

Chapter Sixteen
Personal & Collective
Purpose

Purpose and its meaning…how to connect to more of yours?

I am often in conversations with people seeking to know their purpose. I say your purpose is to love and be loved in return.

I get asked, "Really? That's it?"

I am looking at this gorgeous human in front of me seeking, over complicating their life, over thinking, under valuing themselves, and not recognising their impact. Yet, to acknowledge their gift to others in this life, and all I see is how much they love and how much they desire to be loved in return.

Soul whisper ~ Remember this

"I believe our overarching collective purpose is to love and be loved in return."

In loving ourselves and each other, we open soul paths for one another to live out more purposeful lives. Lives with meaning are more important to us now than ever before. Have you ever wondered why that is? Wondered why more of us than ever before are seeking to live lives that offer more to us than rise, eat, work, sleep, repeat?

In our dictionary, purpose means: "The reason for something being done or created or why it exists"

More than ever, we are having collective conversations around the purpose of our humanity. Asking big life questions like…

- Why are we here?
- What is our purpose?
- Are we here alone?

Of course, these conversations have always existed, yet something is calling us together into an energy, with a momentum of change that no one can deny is present right now.

Without a doubt, in my heart, there is a purpose to us, a purpose to our collective conversation, and a purpose as to why we are all now suddenly more connected than ever before. Every part of our world is connected now and it's visible and real, and quite easy to connect with a sacred human on the opposite side of the planet in a millisecond.

An invisible world wide web of connection which serves and disconnects all at once. Serves us in our connection to soul families across the globe, and new levels of awareness. Truly, little is left unseen. Yet, as with all things Earth-side, the polarity of this connection exists as well.

We are pulled into an invisible web of sometimes false connection. This disconnects us further from our roots, our Earth, the planet itself, and the relationship in real time.

We are at this time on our evolutionary path where we need to make very conscious choices around the purpose of this worldwide connection and what it can gift us. I do feel we must be very mindful of its pitfalls and ability to distract us from truly meeting our purpose in this lifetime.

It is possible that the more time we spend mulling over what our divine purpose is, the easier we will miss it- especially for those on a soul path of remembrance. For, in the mulling over, we miss the connection to the purpose that already exists because we exist.

I talk about us being a living prayer in action. That we are the miracle we are seeking.

I have witnessed so many humans spiral in and around in circles, seeking purpose. All the while, life is passing them by.

Soul whisper ~ Remember this

"Part of our purpose is to be present to the life we are living."

When we live on purpose, we discover more of it naturally. So, what do I mean by living on purpose? I mean that we are here to love and be loved, so part of living on purpose is getting curious and comfortable with seeing all the ways we move away from love.

We are here to feel purposeful, to give meaning to our lives, and to the lives of those we touch. There are so many ways we feel purposeful on a human level, and many of us disregard the simplicity and gifts of our presence in one another's lives.

When I feel into the thread of connection from all the humans I have met, loved, and spent time with, I feel a warmth of loving gratitude wash over my heart. I recognise the purpose we all bring or have brought into each other's lives, even if we are now apart.

I have had friendships come and go and, to this day, I look back with love for our time together and see how we supported each other in reaching towards more of our own unique purpose in this lifetime. I would love to invite humans the world over into the idea that their very existence is purposeful and is valued in the bigger scheme of things.

There is a purpose to our interactions, no matter how short lived. I feel when people these days are reflecting upon their purpose, they are tapping into the collective field of what our purpose is on this planet. I reflect upon questions like. Do we have a collective purpose? Or do we simply arrive, live and die?

I absolutely see the golden threads of connection between us, and our collective purpose being revealed more and more day by day.

We are naturally communal beings who are dependent upon one another for our survival. There are teachings available right now upon our planet that ask us to be hyper independent that say we need nothing or no-one outside of ourselves. Whilst there is a grain of truth to this, it is important to note that this too can be very unhealthy for humans as we are naturally communal beings who thrive best when we work together for a collective outcome and purpose.

It is simply the way we are built. These teachings are asking us to become aware of the ways we are connected through threads of toxicity. The realm of relationship deserves a full book on its own, yet I feel I must touch on it somewhat to gift you the reader some idea of where I am going with this in relation to our collective purpose. Our collective purpose that is very evident the world over right now is to really grasp and become witness to the ways in which we are harming ourselves, one another and this sacred planet that is Heaven on Earth for those with eyes to see.

Never have we had so much information available to us from all dimensions.

This can feel both enlightening and confusing. It can feel and be overwhelming to become suddenly aware as a collective that we are not only human but multi-dimensional in our origins. So many on the planet right now originate from across the galaxies not only this world. If we were all to wake up at once to this collective truth it would be too much to hold for us all.

Which is why, at present, we are seeing all levels of consciousness playing out at once from the lowest vibration to the highest vibration. None are better or more than- it is simply a true reflection of the collective transformation we have all been invited into and are on, whether we are conscious of it or not.

Soul whisper ~ Remember this

"Part of our collective purpose right now is to heal the ways in which we relate to one another, and to meet the

raging wars within us so they no longer exist outside of

us."

That is a personal purpose we all get invited into repeatedly. Not everyone takes up the offer and that is okay. For those of us who do, it is intensely clear how much of our collective dream is being shattered into oblivion to make way for what can be. Some call this time "The Awakening", others "The End of Days", others "The Age of Aquarius". All differently named, met, and understood, depending on our personal purpose and belief systems.

What I see is a collective unravelling of anything and everything that is harming us personally and collectively. I can see how the world right now feels and looks like a frightening place. Yet, what I am witnessed to is a clarion call into a more sacred way of being that honours the divine and the human; the ultimate inner union of what is above and below within the sacred trinity of creation.

Our personal and collective purpose is to unify all in love, within and without. In and around us. This is when we as a collective will know true peace upon these lands. We have a collective responsibility to recognise, or at the very least be willing to explore that there are very real and harmful agendas, both alive on this planet and beyond this plane, that do not want us to know our collective purpose.

I genuinely believe and have said often that the Third World War was never going to be a war of man. It was always going to be a war on the very soul of existence. We are in that time right now and it is intense, challenging, and at times overwhelming for so many.

We are navigating not only our own personal wars within, but the collective shifts that demand our time and attention. Which is why, at present, we have those who are seeing beyond the veils before others, who have been on this path of remembrance. It is not so much about having a hierarchy or that there are those who hold a special power, it is simply that it is part of our purpose to support the collective purpose through sacred conscious leadership until all hearts and minds are open to the path ahead of us.

I ask, "Can you feel the divine thread of existence within it all?"

I can, every day I am witness to it, to this web of light that is wrapped around our planet. In IET we call this a heart net, and the healing Angels who are Raphael, Gabriel, Celestina, Faith, Cassiel, Daniel, Sarah, Michael and of course our beloved Ariel are surrounding it steadily, amongst other light beings who have our collective purpose at the centre of their soul purpose, offering it love to strengthen it as we as a collective move through this transitionary phase in our evolution.

What are we evolving into? "I feel into luminous beings who understand both our human existence and universal existence where we begin to harmonise our inner and outer worlds, and all the knowledge that has existed in past, present, and future timelines."

Humans across our planet are working day and night with timeline grids, both on and off Earth's gridline, clearing energetic forces that have been holding Earth and its inhabitants a prisoner of time.

How are forces holding the Earth and her inhabitants back?

Through continuously looping us in and around …

- Poverty consciousness
- Wars of self-destruction
- Relational abuse
- Power struggles

And by withholding of our universal sovereign rights. We are living in a time where so many truths are becoming known. Some seem so farfetched; they do not feel like a truth to many, yet many more are feeling it and recognising the truths being brought to us at this time of momentous change.

How are we playing our part?

- We are each being giving a piece of our collective puzzle to place down in its rightful place, joining together the dots of confusion.
- We are removing the distortion of the lies we have been told to finally get a fuller view of the picture in front of us.

It is a joyous and a frightening time.

Worlds are quite literally colliding, and we have not fully chosen one or the other. We have our feet in both, dancing wildly in-between, not yet quite centred.

Your very own path of remembrance is a dance in-between, and you will find your centre; we all will eventually. I do not feel we will all arrive at a collective harmonic centre for so many years- hundreds or thousands- I do know I will leave this world having seeded in what I was here to do, and I will return with more to do.

As will so many of us.

Maybe some of you reading this may be wondering what I am talking about, whilst others will be wondering how can you connect more deeply with your own purpose?

I would invite you into reflecting upon the common themes in your life.

To reflect over your lifetime and collect information from the experiences, memories, relationships and identify core themes that are always present.

- What are the causes you feel most enthusiastic about supporting?
- What are the life skills you have developed along the way?
- What has been your most profound learning curves? There will be a common thread within them all.

Something that has been consistent throughout your life that you are passionate about and always present to.

Some examples of ways we serve the collective

- Teaching and/or guiding people.
- Parenthood
- Creativity
- We have the gift for speaking and inspiring others
- We bring a quiet calm into a room
- Kindness
- We may have a way of helping people feel heard and really listened to.
- We may know exactly how to bring joy into the lives of those we meet.
- Speaking truths
- Speaking up for those who cannot
- Tending to the earth, her land, farming

We all have a different purpose, gift, and unique essence within us.

Let us look at my life as an example of how my purpose and gifts were evident since I was a child, readily available for me to use and access.

From as early as I recall, I loved to write, create, paint, and connect with others. I could always feel, see, and read the energy in a room. This was partly through hyper-vigilance due to my upbringing, and I now also believe due to my intuitive gifts. I was very aware of there always being more to this world from incredibly early on and often felt weird and strange with a sense of not really belonging. I struggled with belonging, self-esteem, and worthiness, as well as being crippled with chronic PTSD and riddled with shame. One of my main childhood prayers was that every being find love and peace in their lives. I used to imagine a light flowing through the world into the homes of everyone I knew as a child and teen.

I was already connecting to the web of light that surrounds our planet.

I questioned my Catholic upbringing often yet felt deep resonance with Christ and the devotion to ritual that was witnessed within chapel. I had this untouchable faith that, no matter what was happening in and around me, that people are and always will be inherently good. That we each carry love, even if many forget its presence- even me at times. It is there.

I knew without doubt it is the strongest force of truth on our planet. So, let us look at how my adult life played out… I was continuously brought into experiences that demanded I love myself more. Experiences would get increasingly uncomfortable until I dropped my resistance to the changes my life was asking of me. My life showed me that I had a gift for teaching and bringing people together, and right now it's a huge part of what I do.

My art, my words, and my ability to bring people together for shared experiences all play a part in me living out my purpose. I have come to believe my purpose is to live as a reminder of what is possible, even if life gifted you a hard hand in the beginning. My purpose is to live as a reminder of what it is to call love home to yourself and the world around you repeatedly.

I am here to live a path of sacred remembrance and, in doing that, others remember this for themselves. My purpose is to write and share my heart vulnerably and courageously, even though there is within me huge fears present around judgement and ridicule. A core wound of those of us connected to Magdalene. I am purposeful when

I embody the gifts of my human experience and recognise that not all of it was kind or even of love, yet I am here still able to hold and bring love wherever I go.

My purpose has little to do with being well-known, yet it is exactly what has happened over the years. I have found this part difficult always. There is always a part of me that seeks and prefers to be invisible. If I can leave this world knowing I have gifted a true sense of love and wellbeing even for a moment, I see my life already as one that has been well lived and sacredly purposeful.

I invite you to do the same, knowing that you can in this moment see that no matter what else has played out in your life, you never lost that thread of purpose to love and be loved in return.

Soul gift ~ You are enough

- Close your eyes
- Place your hand upon your heart
- Feel the sensation of your in breath and out breath
- Feel the light of your heart open and begin to fill you
- Begin to affirm out loud-
- "I am enough"
- "I am loved as I am"
- "I am enough"
- Feel the words move into your energy
- Feel them infuse your heart
- Feel them become alive in your energetic field
- Feel this as true
- Know it always has been true

In knowing this,

- You will live your life on purpose with purpose.
- You will live a life of meaning and fulfillment.

- You will move beyond an egoic version of what purpose is
- You will see what has been present all along.

I feel I would be hard pushed to meet a human and not find the presence of love somewhere in their lives. In knowing this, I am inviting you to lift the pressure off with regards to what your purpose is, and to truly drop into the fullness of what is present in your life. Know it is already purposeful from the moment you came into existence.

Soul whisper ~ Remember this

"A life of purpose put simply in a way we can all grasp is a life that has loved and felt love in return."

The more I connected to the purpose of my own existence, the more I began to see how shame was interfering with my ability to be present to the love on offer in this life. We come into this life in a sacred body temple of skin and bones, organs, and muscles. A body that seeks to know love through pleasure.

Chapter Seventeen

Embodying

Pleasure

This body of ours is what moves us and houses the essence of our souls. We choose to come into a body, not so we can ignore it and not feel its gift. We come into a body, into the realms of feeling and sensation, so we can experience the pleasure of being in a body. I have, over the years of this path of remembrance, come home to a place on the inside that knows without doubt that we also came here to experience pleasure in all its forms.

When we are not of a body; we are light energy. We are particles of light with none of the human sensory experiences we get to experience here on Earth. In this body, we get to smell, taste, touch, feel, and access delightful ecstatic wonders of being alive and being human.

We get to feel the density of power that exist within our muscles. We get to feel the sensation of another's skin against our own. We get to feel the breath of life that sustains and holds us between worlds. We get to dance, run, skip, play and feel all the joy of being in a body that wants to experience optimum health so we can enjoy being alive in this world.

I do not believe that we get to experience the richness of a human existence and all that our bodies gift us in other realms. We get to taste nature's existence, the fruits of our land, to feel the movement of our emotions, our felt experience, and a full range of feeling from grief to joy.

There is nothing that cannot be felt within this body. Pain and pleasure co-exist together in this human life, and we are here to experience it all and to feel the pleasure of our existence, of one another. Pleasure gets to be part of your journey home to yourself. Our erotic nature is not limited to our sexual experiences, for the very essence of human life is erotic in how alive and sensual it all is. I find as much pleasure in the beauty of a sunset as I do a sensual kiss. Whilst it enlivens my senses differently, it is still deeply felt and arousing to me. The pleasure that reverberates through my body is not different in terms of what opens in my heart.

As I matured along this path home to myself and began to safely meet shame without fear or judgement, my ability to access pleasure in all areas of my life opened more fully.

So much shifted in my ability to give and receive in pleasurable ways. I began to see that my healing journey did not have to hurt all of the time. That I could play with the energy shifting in my life and feel more enlivened rather than being drained emotionally, mentally, physically, or spiritually.

Yes, there will always be times when the spiral deepens, and we become exhausted by what we are being brought in and through. And right there alongside it is a doorway into a more ecstatic way of being where there is no shame attached to what is being felt. A by-product of this is our ability to connect naturally to a life of pleasure. The more I mature into myself, the more I recognise what is truly available to us. I love being a woman.

There is more pleasure to meet in our lives. The more I grieved what was lost to me as a child, the more I was able to play and have fun in my life. The more I made space for my rage to be met, the more I was able to laugh and be present to joy in ways that were truly felt and authentic.

For many years in my life, I could be in a room full of happy people and be smiling yet feeling nothing and wondering why I could not access the joy others could so freely. A key part to accessing more pleasure in my life was to find ways to be present to the whole of my body, and her every sensation, feeling and experience.

I approached this part of my journey at first with mistrust and a lot of hesitancy, then a subtle, slow trust began to build over time. Until one day I found myself, after a 21-day journey using breath, kundalini, womb connection and prayer, fully feeling the aliveness and sensation of grief and pleasure together.

Full bodied orgasmic energy was flowing through my spine and being. I was being called home to the power of what lived inside of me energetically, that could be felt and met physically- creating better health and wellbeing.

I was being reminded I could be alive to both and all, and that there was nothing wrong with me. I was being invited into the power of my breath and the power of devotion to a daily practice that could open a new level of love for myself and this life path I was here to walk.

It was through this part of my journey that I began to see clearly that I did not need to heal my sexual trauma by revisiting the pain and story continuously. That I could compliment this new learning of breath work, movement, prayer, and ritual with my energy healing practices.

This led to me being curious about other ways we could heal our bodies from the wounds of sexual trauma without reliving traumatic experiences. I was done living out my story in ways that felt depleting and energetically binding to a past I was no longer alive in.

I was done with not being able to access genuine pleasure in my body due to the trauma imprints alive that would be retriggered through a certain touch, smell, or even flashback during my most intimate moments. I no longer wanted to check out of my body so I could orgasm and instead wanted to feel the aliveness of being in my body. My soul was calling me home to this slowly over time.

In this time, it was the wisdom of my womb, the art of ritual, the movement of my body, the sensation of my breath, and the devotion of my prayer that brought me into the sacredness of pleasure repeatedly.

I found the wisdom of yoni eggs first through a sister in circle, then through a mentorship journey online.

What is a yoni egg? It is said we inherited these from the Taoist traditions. A yoni egg is a semi-precious egg shape stone/crystal that we insert up our vulvas. They are known to support our wellbeing and sexual health. There are many kinds of yoni eggs, my favourites are

- Jade egg ~ gifts us connection, sensuality, and pleasure
- Rose Quartz ~ gifts us self-love, compassion and healing
- Black Obsidian ~ gifts us grounding, protection, and clears sexual trauma

7 Benefits to using a yoni egg

- Strengthen and supports our pelvic floor health
- More pleasure and orgasmic energy
- Self-love
- Heals sexual trauma
- Clears our womb energetically
- Relieves symptoms of PMS
- Restores hormonal balance

Soul gift ~ a yoni egg practice

Personally, when I am using yoni eggs, I create ritual. They bring me into the sanctum of self-love and devotion. I am a queen of ritual and devotion.

- I take a sacred bath
- I light some candles
- I select music that works with my sacred intention for the practice
- I anoint my body with my favourite oils
- I have my bedroom clean and clear

- I clear all distractions,
- I choose my yoni egg
- I cleanse and energise your yoni egg

3 Examples of how you can clear and energise the egg

- Hold it in your hand and set sacred intention that it be cleared of any residue energy and then imagine the energy you desire filling up the egg
- Use sacred waters that have been blessed and anoint your egg
- Lay it upon a bed of rose petals and surround it with rose quartz

3 Examples of an intention (please use one of these or something that feels aligned and true for you)

- To clear an old lover out of your womb space
- To clear any blockages to feeling connected to your pleasure
- To bring in more love and compassion

Choose a playlist that feels sensual to you, that will bring you into your body and your turn on

Soul whisper ~ Remember this

"You want to be turned on enough to receive the egg but not quite at the stage of orgasm"

3 Examples of how to reach your sacred turn on.

- Breast massage
- Belly womb massage
- Dancing

3 benefits of sensual self-massage

- Activates oxytocin, giving you a pleasurable and loving yoni egg experience
- Turns you on so you are sexually aroused before using your egg.
- Releases any tension and stress in your body and vagina so you can experience more pleasure.

It is important you are in your body and your body is consenting to this journey. This is especially true if you have been disconnected from your body and unable to identify if you are giving consent or not.

When you feel ready to insert the egg

- Use a lubricator if you need to.
- Insert the egg, wide side in
- Pause at the yoni lips ~ ask for consent
- Pause at the entrance of your vagina ~ ask for consent
- Stay there for a moment to be sure she is open to receiving the egg
- When she enters in fully, don't worry- she cannot get stuck or lost

An exercise to do whilst she is in there

- Move into a bridge pose

Bridge Pose

- Lay on your back arms rested to your side

- Lift your hips up into the air
- As you do this create a root lock- tilt your pelvis, lift your pelvic floor and inhale
- Hold the in breath and imagine the yoni egg pouring her energy into all your womb space
- Drop back down again, resting your whole body on the floor and exhale
- Repeat this a few times until you feel the desire to rest

As you move into the rest position

- Imagine the egg within your womb
- Imagine a golden light expanding from the egg
- Filling your womb, moving through the cervix, fallopian tubes, and ovaries
- Feel your womb like a golden chalice, filling up with the most beautiful elixir
- Until it overflows and spills out, filling the entirety of your body
- Rest in this gorgeous space for as long as you feel to
- Call any excess energy back to the chalice which will stay within your womb space, working on your behalf energetically

To remove the egg

- Pull the string and remove the egg
- Squat down and the egg will pop out
- Surrender into trust and know the egg will release when it is ready

3 Questions I get asked a lot

1. Can it get lost?

No, the cervix prevents the yoni egg from going upwards or disappearing once inside. It will simply rest within the vaginal walls until its ready to release.

2. How do I clean it?

In hot water that has been cooled down to lukewarm or with a safe hygiene product.

3. Can I use it if I have the coil in?

It is not recommended as not enough studies have been done to say it is safe to do so. So, my answer is always no- it is best not to use if you have the coil in.

It's important you purchase from a reputable company and to buy a quality egg. Remember where it is going; your yoni deserves the very best!

I will include some recommendations at the back of this book.

Soul whisper ~ Remember this

"A woman connected to all of life is connected to all of herself"

I suddenly found a world full of women seeking to be present to the pleasure within their own body temples and I had instant soul recognition this too was part of my path. It was part of my homecoming, and part of what I would bring others too in time. My journey was self-led, self-contained on many levels, and very much a solo one. It was not one I invited others into for quite some time or was even open to sharing about.

I found the art of dance call to me- first burlesque, then pole. All of this was a reclamation of embodying my sexual lifeforce in a way that was innocent and playful with no expectation to share it.

I could feel the aliveness of my own unique erotic lifeforce come to life and had an understanding I needed to consciously choose celibacy for periods of time as deep healing happened within my body, womb, and relationship to myself. Which meant having vulnerable conversations about what I needed to let the deep healing happen.

Speaking solely from my own experiences, healing from childhood sexual trauma is …

"Learning to lay with your chosen beloved naked without the need to perform or give anything of yourself to recreate a safety you have never known. Time and time again. It is speaking out loud your fears of truly surrendering into his hands because you have never truly trusted the masculine to take care of you. It is growing up afraid that someday you might wake up and become like your abuser because that is what the statistics say, yet knowing you are not and never will be what he is. It is moving past the physical pain and fear of pleasure that is a very real thing as your body remembers what you have forgotten as you begin to safely reclaim your right to feel in your own body. It is gently beginning a conversation with the parts of your body that are still numb from the experiences of trauma so that you can experience more pleasure in your life. It is choosing celibacy within your marriage/relationship as often as you need to, for as long as you need to, to gift you time to heal and reconnect with your own body in ways only the self can. It is learning to unravel and let go of deeply engrained conditioning that love equates to sexual connection and attention. It is learning to notice and then truly honour when you are saying no internally even though your body is responding with a physical yes, because it has been conditioned to do so. It is vocalising your No even if in the beginning your voice croaks and is barely audible. It is learning to bring into yourself all of the love and compassion you can muster when the parts of you that live in shame, guilt and fear become louder than the love that is real. It is years of unravelling new pathways of safe loving connections that are truly beautiful- honouring where you are in every given moment. It is gifting yourself permission to rage, cry and grieve for as long as you need to."

It is gentle, courageous inner work that I can and will hold your hand through.

I was having vivid memory of how sacred our sexual lifeforce is and being shown the many ways it can often be high jacked upon this planet and misused.

Childhood sexual abuse being a primary hack into sucking our creative life force into an energetic vortex of shame, doubt, confusion, and disconnection. Which serves to keep us in a continuous loop of forgetfulness of how sacred our sexual life force is. Which in turn interferes with conception and our journey into life here on Earth. Sexual abuse is rampant on our planet. It is one of the deepest wounds of our time and is being brought to our attention increasingly as this harm can no longer be ignored. Turning the other cheek simply will not do. If I can stand up to this as a young maiden, then the world can stand against it with a force so powerful that speaks clearly to and for our children. You are safe here with us!

It feeds entities of shame, holding us prisoner to experiences that hold us in the embodiment of shame rather than sacred pleasure. I wish to share an intimate piece of my journey into healing sexual shame and calling home a part of my existence into the arms of love. I was what people would call promiscuous growing up- easy. There were men of all ages not one bit ashamed to approach me, use me, get sexually intimate with me and project their shame unto me. There was a particular group who called me "Guinevere" from the knights of the round table, I can promise you, these were no Knights, and they knew little of respect for the feminine- especially one who was hurting.

And there was another side to this story, a part that grows on the inside of one who has been exposed to sexual harm from childhood.

It is a tricky part to face head on, and often is not spoken to out loud by those of us who have been sexually abused due to the intense shame we feel around it.

I feel it important to bring as someone who holds sacred safe space for many women. I feel it is important I speak to it. To lift the lid of shame and give it no place to hide, for any of us. The shadow of the feminine that lived in me due to sexual trauma was scary to meet and took me to a place within that was both vulnerable and freeing.

An energy developed within my psyche that struggled with saying no and the rejection of a no. As I grew and was often in unsafe spaces and places with the masculine, often of my own choosing, aware that a part of me was doing the harm. The cycles of abuse I grew up in created within me a predatory type of energy that used and manipulated in harmful and destructive ways.

I wasn't always the one being taken. I was seeking and looking to be harmed, and used, in ways that were not healthy or even normal. It would throw my whole being into turmoil as so much of my own desire for love was wrapped up in the warped distortion that love equated sexual connection and attention from the masculine.

A part of me expected to be gazed upon. Wanted it. Sought it. Needed it. Thrived upon men's attention- good or bad- it didn't matter so long as their attention was on me. A part of me didn't know how to stop this part of my expression. It was as if this part of me had a life and energy of its own. Which of course it did. It took years for me to recognise it. To see her, meet her destruction inside of me, her pain, so split I had become from survival.

It was confusing, scary, frustrating, and I cloaked it in fear and shame. This part of me was not necessarily aggressive; it was much cleverer than that. We women know how to use our sexual energy and womanly ways to get what we want, no matter the abuse that has occurred. We know our power and its link to our sexuality, even if it is through a distorted lens through trauma. To face this, is key I believe to our collective healing of the sexual wounding present in our world. For me, this energy played out as needy, manipulative, vixen type energy. To integrate this part of me, and the choices made when it was in full force into loving compassion has been challenging and freeing.

The gateway of devotion work was a pivotal turning point in making peace with this part of my past. This part of me. Understanding the shadow of the maiden archetype guided me through that first gateway and into reclaiming what had felt lost and shameful for me. Had I not met it and owned it, I would not have met the gateways of pleasure that also live right there inside of me now.

I share this piece for those of you who may know this energy and are afraid to meet it. I share knowing that if you don't feel so alone with it, you may find a way to breathe love into that part of you, recognising her actions are or were from a place of deep-seated hurt trying to claw back some personal power from a situation that left you powerless at a most vulnerable time in your life.

There is a whole collective movement around sexuality alive on our planet right now. This is not new, yet it is new to the masses that our sexual energy can be healing, is healing, is sacred. It so much more than orgasms and being aroused for our own pleasure. Whilst there is nothing wrong with our desires and needs to feel and be satisfied in this body, there is something wrong with the sexual lifeforce on this planet if our children are still being harmed through sexual exploitation and abuse.

It is why there is momentum being picked up around healing our energetic hooks to that which would have us stay looping in shame around our longings and desires.

The feminine is aching for the masculine to penetrate her beyond his satisfaction and beyond orgasm. The masculine is aching to be received by the feminine more fully than ever before. This is as much an internal union as it is an external union.

Part of us being able to do that within and around us is to move into the sexual hooks of distortion that are alive on this planet. We live in a world where our yonis (Sanskrit for vulva) have been regulated to that which is profane and pornographic.

Is it any wonder so many of us do not know or understand the sheer power and connection to the sacred holy lands between our legs? We are daily and continuously objectified for the use and service of man. These conditioned belief systems have filtered through humanity and become accepted as normal, leading to a massive disconnection to our feminine essence, bodies, pleasure, power, and healing capacity, as well as our innate womb wisdom.

This disconnection has led us to the separation from our bodily autonomy, and to believe that there is something shameful and wrong with our sexual expression and natural erotic innocence.

This causes so many of us the world over to dismiss our wants and needs sexually, to not have the confidence to ask for what we want and/or need in relationship (not just sexually), and to harbour feelings of guilt, shame, and fear around our desires, and towards our sacred body temples.

It has led to so many not recognising that their own pleasure is as important as the one they choose to offer pleasure to.

We women are made to feel uncomfortable about the flesh over our bones, the curve of our hips, the softness of our bellies. Having our bodies constantly scrutinised and judged has taken its toll on how we show up in our lives, and motherhoods. This is a direct attack on the feminine and it is a direct attack on the lifeforce of our world- the shakti, the womb of creation, eros itself, the Mother of all Mothers- and it is now that we are feeling her call. They may not burn us now, yet we still feel that fire upon our skins!

May we remember, and feel a stirring between our legs, a pulse of recognition as women speak more about what is true for them. May we all experience a sacred remembrance of a time where the feminine was revered and standing by her holy King- undivided and unified- a sacred trinity of loves breath all in one body, in one breath, one moment.

This is what human longing aches for, what it is seeking to return to.

Soul whispers ~ Remember this

"Part of our collective pathway home is to remember her- she who birthed us, the Mother of all Mothers, the cosmic womb of creation, and that she is felt beyond being an object of desire."

For she is you, I, all of us, man, woman, and child. Part of this self-discovery is recognising that pleasure plays a part. To understand that within your womb, hara if you are a man, your sacred body temple, your holy Yoni, lives gateways of devotion that are there to help you access new levels of connection, love, and sacredness beyond the clitoral orgasm. In fact, you will know you have crossed a threshold of sacred exploration when you stop chasing the orgasm (as delicious as they are) and are instead reaching into the heart of your breath and cosmic lifeforce to expand your lifeforce into cocreating a world beyond our wildest imaginations right now.

Your body temple is an exquisite map of ecstasy, healing, and sacred gifts so many of us never reach into. Did you know that your clitoris is linked to your third eye? That your cervix and throat are made similar? That your G-spot is linked to your amygdala? That your womb chalice is linked to your jaw? That your womb collects and holds memory imprints from every lover ever to enter your sacred holy sanctum? That we can become polluted with the energy of lovers- past and present?

That it is important to work with your womb, and sacred anatomy within, to not only clear but energise and store your creative lifeforce?

That working with your sacred anatomy is a gateway, not only to pleasure but to profound healing?

What are the Gateways of Devotion?

Gateways of devotion are a way to connect deeper to our sacred body temples, our inner wisdom, and sacred sexuality. These gateways are an ancient pathway into the embodiment of the feminine mysteries.

The invitation is to take a journey of reclamation so that we get to know ourselves more intimately. They are an alchemical key that activates our eros, our sexual life force into its highest expression.

I am personally fascinated by how interconnected our body is, to that which is sacred and how every part of us is divinely made. I am going to share with you some wisdom to help you connect with the first 3 gateways of devotion and 3 ways you can begin to work with each right now.

What we will explore together

- What each gateway is
- The archetype, season, moon, and womb cycle linked to each gateway
- Where the gateway is in our bodies
- 3 benefits of working with each gateway
- 3 soul gifts within each gateway
- 3 shadow aspects of each gateway
- A practice to work with each gateway

Benefits of working with these gateways of devotion are:

- Deeper intimacy and presence with your own body temple

- Healing of ancient and current life experiences
- A reconnection to your sacred eros
- Deeper trust in yourself
- More confidence in sharing your wisdom and soul gifts
- Ability to speak your truths with greater ease
- More pleasure in all areas of your life
- Access to higher states of consciousness
- Emotional regulation ☐ Heightened intuition
- Spiritual maturity
- Ability to discern what is for you and not for you
- Sacred respect for your body temple
- Courage to walk towards your desired destination in life
- Connection to your creativity

Temple of Innocence

The 1st gate way ~ Temple of innocence

Archetype ~ Maiden

Season ~ Spring

Moon cycle ~ New moon

Womb cycle ~ Renewal

Body wisdom ~ Connected to the yoni lips, clitoris, and thymus gland

3 Benefits of working with this gateway

- Ability to forgive the past
- More trust in ourselves.
- A healthy immune system

3 Soul gifts

- Wisdom
- Playfulness
- Integrity

3 ways to identify if you are in the shadow energy of this gateway.

- A lack of trust in yourself and the world around you
- The energy of fear overrides the energy of love
- You are feeling bitter about life

A soul practice to work with the first gateway

- Sit in womb meditation pose (cross legged on the floor with your hands resting upon your womb).
- Close your eyes and feel the sensation of your in breath and out breath
- Connect with your yoni lips and clitoris energetically (it may help to imagine a pink rose as a symbol of connection)
- Reflect upon these questions
  1. What are you inviting me into in this moment?
  2. Whom and what have I allowed into this sacred space?
  3. What parts in my life are seeking renewal, hope and new beginnings?
- Journal on your discoveries

Temple of Trust

The 2nd gateway ~ Temple of Trust

Archetype ~ Mother / Lover

Season ~ Summer

Moon cycle ~ Full Moon

Womb Cycle ~ Conception ~ Ovulation

Body wisdom ~ Connected to the G-spot and thyroid

3 benefits of working with this gateway

- Supports hormonal balance and healthy metabolism
- More pleasure in our lives
- Opens new levels of compassion

3 soul gifts

- Sensuality
- Passion
- Desires

3 ways to identify if you are in the shadow of this gateway

- Feelings of insecurity
- Low self-esteem
- Body issues and issues with eating disorders

A soul practice to work with this gateway

- Sit in womb meditation pose (cross legged on the floor with your hands resting upon your womb). Refer to womb mudra illustration
- Close your eyes and feel the sensation of your in breath and out breath
- Connect to your G-spot energetically (it may help to imagine a red rose as a symbol of connection)
- Reflect upon these questions

  1. What wisdom does this gateway wish to gift me right now?
  2. What am I desiring to create in my life right now?
  3. What does the truth of my sexual life force feel like?

- Journal on your discoveries

Temple of Wisdom

The 3rd Gateway of devotion ~ Temple of Wisdom

Archetype ~ Crone

Season ~ Winter

Moon cycle ~ Dark Moon

Womb cycle ~ Menstruation ~ Menopause

Body wisdom ~ Connected to our cervix, throat, and amygdala

3 benefits of working with this gateway

- The gift of prophecy
- Deep transformation
- Regulates our stress response to life

3 soul gifts

- Clairaudience
- Power
- Wisdom

Ways to identify if you are in the shadow of this gateway

- Vanity
- You live in the energy of denial
- You use manipulation to get your desired outcomes in life

A soul practice to work with this gateway

- Sit in womb meditation pose (cross legged on the floor with your hands resting upon your womb). Refer to womb Illustration given.
- Close your eyes and feel the sensation of your in breath and out breath
- Connect to your cervix energetically (it may help to imagine a golden rose as a symbol of connection)

Reflect upon these questions

1. What wisdom does this gateway wish to bring my way
2. How connected am I to my feminine essence?
3. What sexual traumas have I experienced in this lifetime?
- Journal on your discoveries

I first discovered that our body holds memory of every experience on a physical, emotional, mental, and spiritual level when I learned the energy therapy IET in 2010.

This healing modality teaches us a cellular memory map process, detailing how our body and organs hold specific emotions, like anger and stress, and how we have the energetic capacity to shift this through specific energetic attunements, which open up our ability to tap into our intuitive gifts and energetically use what we have learned as a diagnostic tool to give us information about where an energetic block is and why it is there.

I believe the energetic work I did for all those years through this healing modality opened enough safety within my body to drop even deeper into the heart of womb work and these sacred gateways of devotion to move into the roots of where my sexual trauma was holding me back from experiencing true pleasure in my body, life and relationships. It is my hope by sharing this that it stirs something in you that remembers and knows your body temple holds keys of power and truth, and that it is perfectly made to reflect the true state of our being in this life.

Chapter Eighteen
Body Wisdom

We are relearning the connection between our body and emotions; our bodies and our mental health; and our bodies and connection to the Earth itself. All of it a divine reflection about where we are, as not only individuals but collectively too.

Where we are in our collective purpose right now is in remembering our body is not in fact separate from the divine. It is divine and it has always been. It is perfectly made for its purpose, our purpose here on earth. Right now, on our planet, there is evidence showing us the clear impact of our choices with regards to how we treat our bodies. Dis-eases that never existed before are existing now due to a lack of knowledge and disconnect to what it is to live in a healthy world.

Others suggest there has been an agenda alive on this planet for some time that has a desire to poison us through our food supplies. To make us ill, docile, and increasingly disconnected to the wisdom of our body temples.

I am of the belief that, no matter what is playing out, there is a force for the greater good that consistently calls us forth into making better life choices, no matter how small they are. We just need to be paying attention, which can be difficult during the unravelling of some of our greatest traumas!

I was once a drug taking, 20 a day smoker, who drank like a fish, lived on my nerves, bit my nails until they bled, and rarely slept. I was paranoid and depressed. I was a woman who ran full throttle on empty, who did not know how to choose health and wellbeing for myself. I watched all the soap operas nightly and read trash magazines. Gossip was normal. In fact, I did not see it as gossip, it was so normal.

I mean, it is easier to tend to another's garden than our own. Yes?

That is what we humans do! Well, no, it's not actually. Healthy secure humans do not do that!

The birth of my eldest 22 years ago in the year 2000 began a shift in me. It would be years later when I would really begin to decide what needed to leave.

Our habitual crutches in life are not so easy to unhook ourselves from. Especially if they were there to support us from feeling or being present to what was seeking to be met inside of us. Our bodies are so clever that, no matter how we treat them, they continuously work hard on our behalf to support our decisions. They will deal with the inflammation, and dis-ease, all the while bringing us to its discomfort.

When I smoked, my body reflected its discomfort through breathlessness and grey skin.

When I stopped smoking, my body rewarded me with more vitality and energy, and I felt the nudge to join the gym. I began to choose better eating habits, I rested more at nighttime, slept better, and did not wake up craving a smoke. I felt less anxious after a year or so of not smoking, even though smoking was something I used to distract myself from feeling anxious. This was almost 17 years ago.

From choosing not to smoke, I gifted my body more breath and more energy. In turn, this helped me relax more into the sensations and desires of what my body wanted and needed. Which, in turn, led to me making more healthy choices. My point being that one small life change can soon spiral into a series of life changes that build upon the other.

All of which, when brought together, gift us more vitality and health within us. I write this knowing my body is not at its optimum health, and I have full awareness of this more than ever before. I know the small steps I must make at this time to build upon the others. I hear my bodily wisdom attune to my heart's wisdom to ask for what it needs so it can be returned to a better state of being. In the past year, I moved through a separation from my beloved and it was hard. The grief was nothing I had ever felt in my life. The feeling of lostness was so vast, I didn't know how to find my feet on the ground. Yet, I had to find my feet alone and fully before I could consider what to do next.

I listened to my bodies need to be still, rest, cry, and not move hard; I let her lead me. I also chose to comfort my big feelings with food.

Foods that have added to me feeling unwell and tired. I am not personally used to carrying a body that feels tired with no energy. It is weird and strange for me to be with my body in this way and I am offering myself the compassion I have spoken to in this book with you all.

Recognising that my body does not want or need to be pushed so hard right now. That she needs gentleness, softness, better nourishment and, when I offer this, the energy and vitality I am used to will return.

This is the healing gift of our body if we are working with it and not against it.

My weight gain is a call to more love. My low energy is a call to rest and more creativity. My awareness of poor food choices is a call back to wellness. My discomfort is a call for more compassion and self-acceptance. A core pillar of my life's purpose is a continuous call to more acceptance and compassion.

I believe when we are truly listening and attuning to the inner whispers of our mind, body, and soul, we live in a way that is naturally pleasurable.

For me, a return to innocence was unravelling all the ways I was stopping love from being felt in my life.

It was walking through gateways of deception I had built up in my life to protect myself from feeling anything. It was the recognition of the fact that there is nothing wrong with me. All my feelings, emotions, and experiences are valid and have served a purpose for me. It was coming home to compassion after years of self-loathing and self-persecution.

It was arriving at the truth that it's not all about me. My behaviour impacts not only my life, but the life of those around me. Especially those I love. It was discovering my body could heal and reattune to an innocent state of being that helped me access new levels of pleasure and ecstasy I did not know was available to us.

It was deepening into prayer and devotion and knowing without any doubt that we are not alone in this life.

Soul whisper ~ Remember this

"Even in our most alone moments, love still lives there and is with us, holding us where we cannot."

It was forgiving myself and others along the way. It was accepting that there will always be parts of me that ache and hurt, and that these parts are the strongest parts of my being. It was in being able to actualise dream upon dream, doing things that I love for the sake of love and not reward or outside validation. For me, my return to innocence was and still is about meeting my sacred ordinary in love, compassion and reverence whilst holding the thread of my divine spirit fully. It is anchoring it to this Earth's plane as we evolve as a species into our most luminous state of existence.

A return to innocence is a return to sovereign truth about who and what we are beyond the cleverly placed veils of deceit that exist upon our planet, blinding us from seeing how miraculous and complete we have always been.

Chapter Nineteen
A Collective Shift

Planetary changes are coming in thick and fast right now. There is a universal reset that is impacting our planet and a global governmental attempt at a reset that is shifting the way we as a world move forwards.

There are vast and fast changes happening all at once and so much of what is present right now in our world simply will be a distant memory come 2032. These shifts are bringing into being new ways of being that are going to impact us on so many levels. I wish to share thoughts on what I feel we will be invited into as the years pass by.

For a while now, we humans have been becoming aware of how trauma impacts our behaviour, and how our behaviour impacts our relational experiences.

Examples of why I believe we are experiencing a collective shift

- We are arriving at states of dissatisfaction within our relationships.
- We are arriving in a place where we are having to get honest about what a healthy relationship is.
- We are beginning to see the ways in which we are trauma bonded

We were not modelled healthy relationships and so this path of discovery is new to us as we navigate and unravel the impact of trauma in our world.

It is an incoming shock for us to see the toxicity of our relationships and patterns of abuse up close and personal. In these moments, we have two choices.

Our two choices are …

- To meet it honestly and seek support
- To deny it exists within our relationships only to have it get more uncomfortable.

Thankfully, we also have conscious leadership showing up for us in this arena across the globe. Move into what feels right for your soul and honour where you are. Do not try to push too hard- being a compassionate witness is important right now. Not making ourselves wrong is important right now.

We are living through a time of revelations, where truths will continue to rise to be met, known, and accepted. From personal to governmental relational dynamics, it is all up for introspection.

Part of that means we will be entering into a time where within our relationships we will be invited into more compassion for the ways we are not holding or honouring one another. It is no accident currently upon our Earthly evolution that there is a rise in relationship and family therapeutic offerings.

We are learning about the polarities that exist in and around us. We are observing our patterns and exploring our attachment styles as we become increasingly curious about why we are the way we are, as well as being more aware that we have purpose- both singularly and collectively.

We are more aware than ever before about how we impact our relationships and what kinds of relationships we want in our lives. We are asking ourselves more and more about what we want from life, family, and relationships.

These shifts we are experiencing, even if some are uncomfortable, are a way through to a paradigm of more ease grace and peace in our relationships and family dynamics.

It is, of course, complex, and personally different for each one of us. Some of us have no desire to shift or change and haven't come to play that role on our planet.

For those of you who are made like me we were born

- To ask the hard questions
- To explore our world differently
- To stay curious
- To unpick the remnants of old

We feel compelled to understand and shift how we do relationship in this lifetime, not only with ourselves but all of life and this planet.

It is like we are rubbing away the stories of old to rewrite a new story, a way of being that invites deep reverence for all of life, not just human life.

Soul whisper ~ Remember this

"How we relate to each other is a direct reflection to how we relate to Gaia, this heavenly planet that is our home."

There is a new wave of hope returning to our planet, asking us to join hands and hearts and to really see one another through the lens of compassion for all the wrongs perpetrated upon us and by us towards one another.

We have lived many lifetimes, met this threshold many times, and fallen many times before. Each time we spiral into our death, we renew and evolve, arriving back at the still point of our new beginning.

Our hearts are aching, and our souls are tired. Yet, here we are, becoming ever more conscious of the dark matter that tries to keep us blind from our ability to choose differently.

The power is in our hands right now. Not much will slip through our fingers if we can hold the energetic sphere of love collectively in place.

Ways we can do that right now.

- Believe it exists

- Tune into it
- Ask daily, "How can I love more today?"
- Pay attention to how we are relating on a human level
- Seek support for ourselves when we recognise our relationship dissatisfaction.

Soul whisper ~ Remember this

"See your dissatisfaction as an open door to more love of self and other."

If you want to know who to watch and learn from, look to the children. A new parenting paradigm is being reborn through the actions of our children who simply refuse to be controlled, coerced, manipulated, or denied their right to be who they are. We parents have our children and have expectations around what family life should look like and feel like, even around how we expect our child to show up in the world.

I am a mother to six. I recall the first book I noticed about parenting sensitive children. My eldest son was seven years old and there were doctors looking to fill him with a cocktail of drugs for his hyperactivity and inability to concentrate. I chose instead to immerse myself in books, knowledge, and information on how best to support myself outside of pharmaceuticals.

It was a challenge, as what it brought me to repeatedly was my own patterns and how my parenting style was disrupting his ability to attune to his own being and inner authority. My oldest boy is an activator, a disrupter by his very nature. What do I mean by that? I mean his energy has the kind that walks into a room and triggers the big people around them into their shadows just by his presence, his joy, his probing questions, and his inability to sit still. He had a gift of bringing us to what we needed to look at and deal with to be a better parent, to ask questions, and to explore other ways of connection. Had it not been for him, I would not have picked up my very first parenting book.

I love him deeply for this. I also found his invitation extremely hard as it meant diving into my own shortcomings. None of us like us in our worst light. Right? I am not alone in that, I am guessing. I have since become a mother to four more bright stars. Here is my thoughts and feelings on today's children. My younger three are wild and spirited, much more than my elder children, or it is possible I am much more relaxed about gifting my children more room to truly be themselves with much less interference.

A Soul gift ~ Wisdom on today's children

Today's children are born

- With their full sovereignty intact and a high level of awareness around this fact.
- With a high resistant to systems which serve to control, manipulate, or have power over them.

Parenting these children requires such an elevated level of mental, emotional, and spiritual awareness if we are to meet these children where they need to be met. So, they can indeed fully flourish and grow beyond that which tries to control them into submission.

It is part of why there has been a mass remembrance of our divine soul parts for those of us who are now parenting these children.

Today's children, particularly those born from 2005 onwards, are an uncontrollable generation of quite honestly genius children, who are born to challenge every system of control in ways no other generation has before.

Right through from parental to governmental. Which is why the old school, authoritarian, and coercive style of parenting or educating of these children simply will not work.

They are also potentially going to be the most misunderstood children of our time as they breakdown systems of separation and harm.

These children can and will create the change the generations before them have prayed into being. They do, however, need us the adults to shift our perspective and begin to unravel the hierarchy of control within us. To heal the deep wounds from not being trusted ourselves as children.

I honestly feel and see how much an adult trusts in themselves by how much trust they place in the children around them. The children of today's world carry ancient wisdom. Often you will converse with these children and find it hard to believe they are a child, as these tiny sages reveal truths that shatter our illusions.

I listen to them speak and the topics of conversation are often deeply profound and teaching us something if we are open to listening. These children are so self-aware, and yet so young. They know how to express their needs and wants and can articulate quite well what they are feeling and why. There are inverted teachings upon our planet that have existed for thousands of years now being seen for what they are.

I look around and see so clearly what the children already know. They are here for another world, a world not yet built, a world that lives out of reach yet is coming into being.

It is their care givers, teachers, and parents (I include myself here) that need the teachings.

I invite you to sit in silence and observe the children around you for a day. Pay attention to them beyond their ego and witness the ways in which they show up. Observe and pay attention to the ways they tend to life and each other.

It is such a gift to witness.

What is happening that is harming today's children is the fact that we are ignoring their quite vocal requests for autonomy and freedom from systems and experiences they know are harming them on so many levels.

We are in this world between worlds, still trying to force our children into a world they do not belong, nor feel truly part of, leading so many of them by the time they reach nine or ten years old into emotional, mental, and physical breakdowns. These children are New Earth children: crystal, diamond, star, and indigo.

These children are highly attuned to world issues that are affecting, not only humanity, but the Earth and all sentient life. Many of them will become enthusiastic about world issues that triggers their heart's soul call and activates their purpose much younger than many of ours showed up for us.

These children are highly capable of self-led learning, if given the space, trust, and freedom to do so.

So many of these children express a desire to be at home, as so much of our educational systems are highly insensitive and ill equipped to fully support them.

They are overly sensitive to foods, certain smells, touches, energy, people and what they perceive as untrue.

It is important we learn to listen to the children so we can cocreate environments for them to thrive in. They are so highly intuitive and feel so much more than their system can hold at times, to the point the environments they are in are simply too overwhelming for them to feel at ease in.

They love nature and will thrive being immersed outdoors often and plenty. We need to be reminding these children how to protect, shield, and work their own energetic and emotional field.

Helping them understand their own energy bodies so they can comfortably relax into this world as it breaks through to the new world, they came to be part of. It is extremely uncomfortable for them here in this in-between world.

These children are receiving diagnostic labels, which matter and are important for some right now as we dance through these transitional times from the old world into the new.

It is helping us create compassion and take action to support them through the daily difficulties felt and experienced by these incredibly wise souls that have arrived onto our planet; some for the very first time.

These children play a part in the crumbling of the old to make way for something much more nourishing and sustainable for our future.

The schooling system is not the only system of repression. Our banking systems are corrupted, our food supplies are depleting in the nourishment needed to sustain good health, family structures are breaking down, and our working environments are vastly over pressured and stress inducing experiences. We have a controlled governance that does not adhere to universal law and continuously overrides our sovereignty and right to a life of thriving purpose.

This veil of deception has been lifted and we are seeing the ways in which controlled agendas exist to have us continuously looping in stories of lack, fear, and scarcity. Turning us on one another, feeding the story of divide and separation.

We must learn to trust ourselves and each other. To trust what is inside of us. What is guiding us to make the changes in our lives, in our relationships, in our health and wellbeing is bigger than us, and for us. Trust it, especially if it seems like you are going against the grain, or standing on the outside looking in.

Trust you are on the outside for a reason.

These systems that have been in place have slowly, over time, enslaved us into dying and rebirthing into traumas of old, spiralling patterns continuously. They have moved us into harming each other, sentient life, and the Earth herself.

Our world cannot and will not hold as it is, as we move towards our sacred evolution. Which is happening, whether you believe in it or are consciously active in it. It is happening. Now is the time.

There is no more time. What we decide today matters. Every choice you make matters. Every time you choose not to trust your instincts will matter and have consequences. Every time you choose to follow what is comfortable because it is easier, will have a consequence.

We were made for these times. We have been in the underbelly of our own self-importance for many years and have been active in our journey to unpick the hooks of distortion that would have us believe one is higher than another on this plane of existence. We are equal in that we are all worthy of safety, love, health, wellbeing, nourishing relationships and so much more. We are unique in that we each stand sovereign in our own unique essence and have something that only we can gift.

We will meet fear as the systems of repression fall- our health systems, our monetary systems, our food supplies- many will move into hysteria. They will feel like they have been taken off their mothers' breast and now have no tangible substance to feed them.

What I believe in my heart is this

- We all made our choices on where we would land when this change arrived.

- We all already know on a soul level the part we are choosing to play in the grand design of our great remembrance.
- All will be celebrated eventually until then it will feel like a world of wars.

This is and will continue to impact us on a psychological, mental, emotional, and spiritual level. There is a war between worlds and all of existence, right now, as Gaia takes her throne upon this universe.

It is messy, but life is messy. This will stay messy for a while as we figure it all out together, even if we are feeling very alone in it all.

Soul whisper ~ Remember this

"Find your people, love them, and grow with them." Anchor in your energetic blessing to our new Earth gridlines by being who you came to be.

What I am sharing will arrive as it needs to and those with ears to hear will meet it as it is intended. Whilst there may be an agenda to disrupt the world and move humanity into a constant state of fight or flight, I am asking that you listen deeply and feel deeply what I am about to say.

This fall of all that has been unsustainable, particularly here in the west, will serve us all, for we will be forced to look at each other eye to eye and heart to heart, and truly lean into supporting one another.

How do I believe this will serve us:

- We will become more conscious of who we spend our time with
- We will pay attention to where and to what we extend our energy towards
- We will choose more consciously how to live, and where we choose life.

- Our values will become less about serving the mighty "I" and we will leave behind the old battles that have separated us for a millennial.

We will reach a state eventually where we will choose to collectively co-create and consciously evolve together.

I am unsure if I will see this fully land in my lifetime, I simply know it as true.

There are still so many choice points available for us all. I imagine there will be many realms of existence all playing out at one time until we harmonise into a collective soul song.

There is already a worldwide choir of Earth Angels and warriors singing a new way of being into the very fabric of our existence. Sometimes I dream about it. I see the vision so clearly. In this moment I am recalling a dream I had once. I was all golden and sparkly, and everywhere I went a gold glitter dust trail was left. My skin sparkled. I was pure golden light.

Everyone could feel the light. It was breathtaking to witness myself like that and it was one of those dreams that felt as real as waking life. I woke up knowing this is what we feel like to one another when we are in our fullness. This dream was a vision of our future selves. This golden light, crystalline, for me was Christ-like energy, love's vibration. This dream was about hope, like this book is.

It is the kind of hope that cracks us open and helps us make peace with and highlights what in our world is simply not working. In our world right now, anything that is not aligned in the truest vibration of love is up for evaluation, elimination even. None of it personal, yet all of it so personal, and necessary. What must go, must. Patterns, behaviours, relationships, beliefs, and old harmful ways of existing. I see Archangel Michael with his sword of light, standing by Christ, and cutting away everything and anything that is not fully supportive of our sacred evolution.

It is quite literally in our faces, uncomfortably so. So glaringly obvious that it cannot be ignored. The ways in which we harm each other will continue to become known, in our individual experiences and globally.

These are golden keys of opportunity being gifted to us to step up and out of our own ways, into new ways of being and new ways of relating.

This will create more space for

- Honesty
- Compassion
- Understanding
- Freedom
- Passion
- Respect
- Love

Love is really what it is all about! It is that driving force that keeps us coming back to this beloved realm of existence. This force of love is all that truly matters.

When we pass through beyond this life, all that will matter is how much have we genuinely loved?

It is a potent time to reflect upon the ways we withhold love from ourselves and each other. From our planet.

It has never been more important to stand up for us, for those we claim to love, for our greater communities and the vast global issues that are screaming for our attention. We are all feeling it. We are all seeing it. We are all living together through these times, where turning the other cheek simply will not do. Where home comforts and distractions will become less appealing.

For you see, ignoring the obvious pain and broken pieces in our world is simply not an option anymore. We are on this great path of remembrance together, having chosen this time to be alive. We have chosen to become witness to our greatness and our most insidious actions.

There are those of us who know we have been called to serve; others' may be feeling it for the first time.

Imagine if we all felt and answered our heart calls into action right now. Imagine if we all took the actions, we were called to within ourselves, our communities and society. We would meet this time of great revelation with hearts open and hands held together. We would make this momentous shift and awaken within our hearts a way of being, ensuring the festering within humanities existence had nowhere to hide and could do no more harm.

The greed, corruption, and abuse that hijacks our very peace of mind and heart would dissolve and we would rise and be golden, just like my dream. Light would fill every pore. I know and trust within my heart that we are all divinely sent and made for this time. Each playing our role.

Imagine if you will that we are in the labouring stages right now. It is painful and beautiful all at once. Many worlds in one world. Many choices and paths being revealed. Mostly to be with fear or love. Choices that will lead to more suffering than necessary; others will ease suffering. We have a choice in every moment.

Every day we have a choice. To suffer or not suffer. To create more suffering or less. We are sweating out the old. Let it go. Sweat it out. Scream it out. Dance it out. Paint it out. Sing it out. Find your way to let it go, and do it, every day if you must, for as long as you must.

We are also pushing prematurely before we are fully ready to expand and truly birth our rightful place back into this world.

You are wondering why is this so painful? Partly because it is, it's human life; this life was never going to be free of pain. I invite those of you who are feeling it intensely right now, to stop pushing so hard.

Try trusting in divine will, not your will. When we women, for example, push at the wrong time while labouring, too soon, we tear ourselves open as we go against the nature of our bodily wisdom and breath.

If we are going against the nature of universal divine law by pushing our personal agendas and expectations to the fore, we will be called on it. What we build will crumble and fall if not in sacred alignment with new Earth energy. I get it- we are sometimes forgetting to breathe and trust, making our ancient new world decisions in old world ways.

Right now, Gaia feels who is being led by heart. We are interconnected to her and all that exists upon her. Seen and unseen, all is truly known and seen.

The only people we hide from is ourselves! Gaia knows what she is doing. The question is, do we?

The universe knows what it is doing. The question is, can we open our minds to its wisdom?

The Divine Mother knows what she is doing. The question here is, can you feel her, remember her name, and hear her call?

Ancient Wisdom runs through our veins as old as time itself. It ruptures through our bodies like holy hell fire with one soul intention- To burn through anything and anyone that dares to claim Holy innocence.

She wisdom invites us home to more peace, a deeper love, and sacred compassion. It whispers truths emblazoned upon our skins for safe keeping until the time comes here the words beneath your skin become alive again.

Full bodied urges scream from the inside out- Speak up woman!

Let us hear you, let us see you, let us know you.

Woman, as you are. She lives and breathes in you, in me.

Shekinah, Shekinah, Shekinah. Heart sound of our existence, creator of life. maker of blood and bones, and Temple of light.

Sophia, Hathor, Isis, Mary, Magdalene. In servitude and gratitude, Holy Thou art thy name. Thy will be done. For He that made us knows we are not priestess, we are not Goddess, we are not mystics, witch, nor angel with wings.

We will be stripped bare to the bone. step out of old skins, lay upon his altar once again, an ecstatic remembrance, offering love back to source. In prayer, devotion, and ritual.

Naked, enlivened, activated, holy, innocent, divine, miracle-Woman. As she was born to be in this body, blood and bones, heart, and soul.

Woman, who is sacred. she who births creation, awakens dreams and who is visionary. In tune, attuned, aware, enough as she is.

Ancient whispers, threads of her existence weaving inner strength body, mind and soul.

Woman in this body. blood and bones, heart, and soul. a vision of delight. Feet upon the Earth, dancing with the moon, alive, wild heart, singing holy her human song.

We need no title to feel worthy, to be woman. Woman, you are enough. Remember her name, hear her call, she lives and breathes in you, in me.

Shekinah, Shekinah, Shekinah Heart sound of our existence, creator of life, maker of blood and bones and Temple of light.

Heart and soul. Bridget, Joan of Arc, Quan Yin, Kali. Perfectly made, divinely held, no more seeking, no more hiding woman.

Woman standing strong, she who awakens and stirs those asleep, birthed in the heavens, born of the Earth. Firmly rooted, open hearted, fully present and a source of light.

She who is an activator of inner sight, leading us to what lays hidden... Slowly, tentatively, compassionately.

Woman. enough as she is looks, sees, believes, knows that she is enough, and worthy of deeper love, for she lives and breathes in woman.

Shekinah, Shekinah, Shekinah, heart sound of our existence, creator of life, maker of blood and bones and a Temple of light.

I am that I am.

I am woman,

Enough

As I am.

The Sacred Mother has no care for those of us who believe ourselves to be right, and only in those that are led by our hearts.

Know the Divine Mother knows what she is doing. Know that the universe knows what it is doing.

Our lost faith is not a reflection of her uncertainty, it is reflection of ours.

I understand many in our world are looking on, bewildered, and wondering what in the hell is happening as more of our holy hells reveal themselves. Cults of old will die, religious faiths that have captivated souls in spirals of guilt and shame to control and undermine their true connection to that which made them will show themselves true.

Many already have. Churches hiding behind a false faith have been shown to be a church of many atrocities, harming our children through sickening abuses and crimes against humanity, especially women, including the death of our children, mass graves worldwide and many more yet to be discovered.

With each spiral of sickening truth, we will move through both personal and collective cycles of rage, shame, disgust, and grief, leading to more and more hearts opening to wanting to stand for truth.

This time of revelation will show us some of the worst crimes against humanity and our sovereignty. It will be harder than not as we bear witness to some of the worst horrors. It will not always be pleasant viewing, yet we must see, so that we cannot unsee. For it is those moments we choose something better for all! I understand that we have not all fully met with our divine mothers' holy surges as she births us into our fullness.

Some of us have, some of us never will, some of us are only meeting her now in recent moments of our lives.

What will be helpful as we navigate these times together is this

- Know our evolution is happening.
- Know we are not alone in it.
- Be a co-creator and consciously active in it.
- Know we have a collective energetic wave of power at our disposal to bring great shifts our way.
- Know our world is purging what is no longer sustainable for our greater good, and yes, we do not yet know if that includes humanity, us, if we will stand the test of time in this grand remembrance.

That has yet to be revealed and our actions or non-actions play a role in it. The power is in our hands.

The key to our everlasting freedom, dare we seek it, to our Garden of Eden, to our Heaven on Earth existence, to be our fully luminous selves, is to remember our divinity and unify it fully with our humanity.

We will simply vibrate differently. We will open our inner Heaven and Earth essence. We will open our hearts and eyes to what lays within, helping us anchor in and express our sovereign energetic essence.

Soul whisper ~ Remember this

"We will continue to rebirth ourselves, despite what reveals itself in the cracks of our Earthly existence."

To believe will get us there with more ease, more are reconnecting to their soul whispers daily, in the years to come you will hear many speak and share their visions for a holy Earth, of our resurrection.

It will birth a new era of sacred leadership upon these lands, welcomed leadership, leadership that understands the medicine of a full circle, of being together in a circle with the world and its people.

A communal governance that honours feminine and masculine leadership as one body, one temple, one light to hold and sustain all.

Sacred leadership will be needed, is needed, until it is not, and we are living in harmony.

I feel and see conscious sacred leaders in this world, leading us through all the portals to our unification of divinity and humanity.

I feel it ungrounded to believe that we do not need support, guidance, and to be led through these times we find ourselves in.

Of course, we do. It is why since the 1990s there has been what some call a quickening to open the energetic forces needed to awaken more of us to our own path of remembrance so we can clearly see our part at this evolutionary time. To support those who would wake up from their own soul slumber, one heart at a time. Without leadership and the embodiment of what is possible, we would not be sparked open to receive what we need to align with our own personal soul path of remembrance.

Some examples of sacred leadership right now are:

- Those embodying better health and vitality in their bodies

They are supporting us into becoming healthier versions of ourselves, minus all the pollution we put into our bodies. Reminding us through their embodiment of what the human body is capable of.

- Those teaching us about conscious relating

They are leading us through the relational crisis each will face as we meet our personal and collective trauma of the original separation from the love that made us.

- Visionaries who feel a world beyond this world

They are here to lead us into our path of remembrance by living out loud theirs for all to see and recognise as a soul nudge from source, which in turn will intuitively guide each of us to the right mentors and guides for our growth and wellbeing at this time.

- Those embodying and teaching about sacred sexuality

They are a living embodiment of what is possible within the realms of sexual exploration in human form.

- Those who tend to and farm the lands ethically

They are our Earth keepers who know and understand her more intimately than most.

- Artists and creators

They are a continuous reminder of our ability to create something out of nothing that evokes something from within us.

Here is what I believe to be true: Source, Creator, I like the word God, does not want us to suffer or struggle in life, in relationship, in health, in our purpose, or our communities. Sacred conscious leadership will bring into our lives people at destined times to help us along our way. It is like the time I met my dearest friend and soul sister Michelle. Which has nothing to do with sacred leadership and more to do with a soul moment with destiny. We were doing a math's class, both of us uninterested yet required at the time to further our chosen career path.

Our connection was sparked through a dislike of math, yet our soul paths brought us together at a time when our whole worlds were colliding and opening up in new ways.

Little did we know how much we would lead and support one another in such a sacred way as we discovered more of our own soul path of remembrance. This is an example of destiny taking care and bringing us what we need. I am sure, if you were to stop and reflect right now, you would be able to identify certain relationships and timelines that were significant and supportive at a time of profound change in your lives.

I believe these moments to be predestined and part of the divine plan that continues to invite us to collaborate with it more consciously. Which is what sacred conscious leadership is, as well as part of the divine plan supporting us to evolve beyond the stories of old.

Currently in our world, it does take a certain quality of divine human to show up and truly honour, hold space, and love us all home again. We are blessed if we have these people in our midst, guiding us through these stormy times. I know and feel that we do not all need to be awake necessarily to be present to what is holy and sacred within. It may feel mentally, emotionally, physically, and spiritually heavy at times to be with all that is being brought to us right now. The feminine principle seems to be the one going first. Know there is a hidden jewel that is present within all men that is being activated daily. Not all who claim to be "awakened" are truly conscious and not all who think they are consciously leading through the heart are fully awakened. A new balance of trust is enveloping us all. It matters not who steps up first, or who knows what when. It only matters that we do step up for ourselves and each other.

One by one we will unveil the most sacred divine expressions of our soul's light and gifts, right here and now. We will remember, we will release what is not needed, we will reclaim what is rightfully ours, and we will return to more of our innocence as we walk each other home on this sacred path of remembrance.

We are still learning. Not all light work will feel light- its light is intended to rupture anything on the outside that is not fully aligned with what is happening on the inside. Relationships are furnaces of transformation. We humans can find this hard to accept; we tend to cling onto the old. We are being divinely led to those we vibrate similarly to, enriching each other's lives. We are learning that we do need to lean in towards each other and move beyond the programs of separation that have been stopping us from creating bridges of peace on this planet.

Much of what is ending is making space for conscious sacred leadership to rise out of the ashes of our turmoil. It will take time. We are soul tired. Tired of hurting. Tired of fighting. Tired of all the ways we harm. We are recognising the changes we are seeking begin within us, to impact around us. It begins with us. It ends with us. One human heart at a time. We are as sacredly ordinary as we are divine. We will be more able to discern what true leadership looks and feels like. This is an exhausting cycle of rinse and repeat we have been in for a millennia. It is okay to question the authority upon this planet and ask what is truly leading you. Are you content with where you being led to, or are you hearing the soul call of our collective hearts and answering its call?

What I have full faith in right now:

- I have full faith in humanities' collective heart resonance that enough is enough.
- I have full faith that we are the bridge between what separates us.
- I have full faith that those walking the Earth right now are made for these times.

It is not an easy path we have chosen.

To bridge one paradigm through to the next level of our evolution. It was never going to be easy. Know our evolution is underway and has been written in the stars for an exceptionally long time. We are walking each other home. One heartbeat at a time. It makes sense you are losing faith in our political leadership right now. It makes sense we are seeking out communities that hear our personal heart calls for change. It makes sense you feel some fear as we dance in the in-between. We will look back at these times and see it all. One of the most powerful things you can do right now is spend time daily in faith, envisioning and re-imaging our world anew. Turn off the noise, get outside, play with the children, swim in the oceans, dance in the rain, laugh and tap into joy. Remember the love that lives and breathes in you. It is our greatest gift to one another now and always.

Chapter Twenty

Feminine Leadership

What is sacred feminine leadership?

Here I will list a few examples of what I believe feminine leadership to be:

- It is women who lead from the heart.
- It is women who are genuinely interested in connection, community, and collaboration.
- It is women who understand what it means to sit in circle- eye to eye, heart to heart, and womb to womb.
- It is women who are pregnant with all of life and connected to all of life.
- It is women moving beyond their deep-rooted fears of being seen in their gifts.
- It is women who understand what it is to be held and to hold.
- It is women who know what it means to listen without fixing.
- It is women who honour their path of remembrance
- It is women who understand what it is to choose a life of devotion
- It is women we naturally feel safe to be around
- It is women who actively seek conscious leadership and mentorship on a soul and human level.
- It is women who can and are moving through their fears of mockery, judgement, and being misunderstood (a deep-seated Magdalene wound)

They are often on the outskirts of their communities locally, even their families; some might say the outcast of society.

These women fully recognise and see the spiritual urgency beyond the veils of this world to begin to show up, act, and most importantly to be seen and visible in their light. So that those who are seeking their wisdom can find them. We are here to serve, love, heal and be present to the collective shift. We are moving out from the shadows so that we may all see one another. We are the healers, herbalists, witches, shamans, holy women, seers, mothers, the medicine women, dream weavers, the Magdalene, Sisters of the Rose, womb and heart, and the soul whisperers of our time.

You know who you are.

You feel the call deep within you that you are here to serve beyond ordinary life.

We are carrying deep wisdom and knowledge from across the galaxies and lifetimes here on Earth within us. We are singing our songs aloud so that they are heard.

We are the women who have been shredding through unhealthy attachments. We are the women who know what it means to walk into the dark- naked, raw, and vulnerable.

We are the women who are consistently rising, stronger and more empowered than before, through the holy flames of our inner transformations, born anew. We are the women others may secretly despise because we trigger that part of them, they have yet to see and reclaim as their own.

We are the women who have been shamed for being too sexual and claiming our bodies and its pleasure as our own.

We are the women who know what depths must be met, and who face our fears head on- even if shaking- leaving us embodying a certain kind of magic that opens curiosity in others.

You are the women who root for other women, knowing the gift it brings to us all.

You are the women who know the time is now.

To be seen.

To share.

To lead women home to the leadership that lives in her.

Your initiations are tough- ripping through all that is untrue so you can meet what is true.

Each sacredly ordained by the divine.

The world needs you now. Needs your sacred gifts. Your full presence and power open and flowing effortlessly.

You will need to learn to get comfortable with being judged, misunderstood, disliked, and talked about, so that you can guide, protect, love, gift and heal. You understand this sacred path of remembrance is not something you find, for it finds you and reminds you that you are the ones we have been waiting for. We are here around the globe in our tens of thousands, receiving our soul's invitation to remember. Opening our hearts to service beyond ourselves and creating safety wherever we go. We are finding our women, creating circles, spiralling outwards, seeding in hope.

If you do not have a circle of women, find them. Invite them into your life. Set the intention to find one, locally or online. You will remember together, open together, blossom together, claim and find the power of your voices, and magical things begin to unfold. In our lives, relationships, businesses, in our world, our spirals ripple outwards. We feel the call of nature and understand we are interictally connected to her. In our connection to her, we rediscover not only our wildness, but we also find our innocence too.

We know that every time one of us speaks up, every time one of us walking this path of remembrance releases that which she must, every time we reclaim our sovereignty, we arrive home to more of sacred leadership gifts; bolder, wiser, braver, softer, and stronger all at once.

We will stop trying to escape this world, stop numbing ourselves with our chosen poison, stop giving of ourselves to connections that do not fully honour us, and we begin to co-create communities from our hearts not our egos. We feel the wisdom of the ancients and rise in confidence, sharing more of our essence with ease and courage.

Those who need our unique soul presence find us, and us them, together we grow. We learn that our gifts are not ours to hold. For to hold them is to withhold our creation itself from this world. We lead from a place that empathises with our humanness, understands what is broken, clearly sees our need to be loved, seen, heard, valued, and met. Sacred leadership understands and learns to appreciate what is less lovable with compassion rather than disdain.

We flourish and feel inspired to take our sacred services out into the wider world. As we walk ourselves and each other home, we no longer fear the death spirals and welcome them in, understanding the thread that is unravelling will be woven into the golden nectar needed for us to continue this path of service to which we are committed. We embody a certain strength with an otherworldly essence that people are naturally drawn to, or at the very least curious about. As it reflects to them their own sacred stirrings, calling them home to more of themselves.

Right now, across the globe, there is a red thread of hope being woven through the hearts and wombs of women who are pregnant with life, vision, beauty, expression, connection, and wisdom. These women can move past the shadows of their own insecurities, fears, resentments, competition, and jealousies into celebration of one another. They are shifting their experiences of pain into expressions of radiance and pleasure. They hold soul keys of sacred remembrance on how to restore humanity to its original holy innocence, past the generational curses of the past. These sacred women know how to hold the masculine in love as he too moves through the rumblings of destruction from history. We have gifts that guide, protect, and soothe the ache and longing for deeper connection to all of life. We can safely feel the rage of the ages erupt and clear the path ahead.

Each of us carrying sacred medicine for her soul family, soul-purpose, and sacred land we choose to root into. We access this for ourselves by being ourselves- recognising we are enough, and always have been.

Sacred feminine leadership knows how to hold, not only her own power and vision, but she also knows how to hold others too, until they can hold all that is seeking to emerge!

Chapter Twenty One
Collective
Soul Whispering
Session

I asked women from my community for questions they wished to have answered by the Angels and guides that walk with me on my path of remembrance.

Together we will answer your soul questions.

1. When will world hunger end?

"World hunger ends when greed and corruption no longer exist on the earthly plane. World hunger reflects the corruption that exists within the false hierarchal systems of power that govern our world."

I ask how we can assist in clearing greed and corruption.

"The answer is we seek to meet that in us which takes more than we truly need. We reflect upon our own integrity in all that we give and receive and get into right alignment with what is fair and honest, and become impeccable with our word and actions. We are moving into a time where nothing can truly hide, where all is and will be seen. This is an uplevel in consciousness which will serve to bring us all into better alignment so that all are cared for fully. There are and always have been enough resources upon Earth to care for all who inhabit her. This will be known, and all will benefit."

2. What else is possible?

"Everything is possible as Earth and humanity find its way home to the fullness of what is truly possible. Humanity is at a crossroads and is currently being flooded with what some of you call light codes, which is higher consciousness making itself known.

You are coming to learn, understand and know that you are not alone in this universe. That there are allies here to support your evolution and sacred remembrance.

Many are waking up to their soul's purpose to assist Earth as she makes this transition into claiming her throne.

What is possible is as wide as the ocean is deep.

What is possible is a humanity that knows there is enough for all.

What is possible is a return to what you call Eden.

What is possible is a reconnection to your universal star families and collaborations that will support one and all.

What is possible is telepathy, language without words, a humanity that understands its role universally, who understands themselves as cosmic beings of light with great powers that can and will heal instantaneously dis-ease as it arises.

What is possible is a humanity in harmony with the Earth, with one another.

What is possible is a humanity that begins to see the sacred technology that exists within your body temple, and how to work with it more fully so that you reach optimum health, eradicating dis-ease altogether.

What is possible fully depends on what you choose to move into as a divine sovereign and collective source of love."

3. Will the world/collective see and get to interact with other beings from other planets in this lifetime? Will everyone experience this?

"Your world is seeing and interacting with other beings right now. Governing bodies are interacting with beings not from your planet. Souls from all around the world are bringing you information to support you. These connections are available to you all, always. Before you arrive Earthside, you are assigned guides, what is known as a Council of Nine to support your evolution. These guides are specifically chosen in accordance with your current life lessons, karmic blueprint, and sacred soul journey at this time for you.

These guides are linked to your soul's energetic blueprint and part of your star family. They may consist of light beings who have never been on the Earth plane and those who have lived incarnations upon Earth. Some may be from your ancestry; others will be chosen because of their specific skills and knowledge they have attained through their own evolution.

Other beings can and do connect with you to support you through specific shifts at pre-destined times. You always have the sovereign authority to ask who is connecting to you, and why. You also have the divine sovereignty to refuse support and help on your Earthly path. Right in this moment, you are connecting with me, another being of light who does not live upon your planet. You feel us through your body, through sensation, thoughts, sounds, and/or a feeling, through what you call intuition. To answer your question- will everyone feel and meet other beings form other planets in this lifetime? Yes, everyone is always connected to and experiencing other beings as you do not come alone to experience this life. You are continuously supported, even if you are not feeling it. Know that we are here."

4. Are we close to coming together to save our planet? Or are most of us not ready to understand and accept the changes we need to make personally, as a community, and globally to make that happen?

"Your question implies that Earth needs saving. Gaia knows what she must do to find harmony within the universe.

In this moment, we wish to offer you another perspective, one that invites you to open your mind- to see that many realms exist within Gaia. She is so much more than a home for the human experience; she is a planet that can hold many realities and beings- both seen and unseen all at once. Once you see this and know this to be true on your home planet, you begin to open to the endless possibilities of what can coexist all at once. In knowing this, you are being offered a gateway to feeling more at ease about your chosen incarnation and experience at this time, alongside your chosen role in supporting Gaia at this potent time universally. Many eyes are upon Earth at this moment, and it is glorious to witness humanity come home to its power and sovereignty on a planet so rich and diverse in its experience. Fear not, for Gaia is coming home to the seat of her power and her guardians know their roles."

5. Will patriarchy be healed?

"This system of control has greatly harmed Earth, sacred union, and your relationship to the Earth itself. Its hold is releasing slowly as you all begin to remember what it is you are here to do. To answer your question- yes, patriarchy will heal, balance will be restored, and safety will return over time as bridges of trust are formed."

6. How can we make the most out of our incarnation, not just for ourselves but the whole of humanity?

"On the Earth plane, one makes the most out of their incarnation when they recognise that a human life is a most valued part of a soul's evolution. To live, breathe, and be housed within a physical body is a sought-after experience by many universally, and not all are chosen. How you can make the most out of your individual incarnations is to be present to the life that is yours. To not seek to live your life as others do. To spend time seeing each day as a gift, a gift that you get to open, and unwrap for your benefit. For every human that see's and recognise their unique life as a gift benefits the whole, as they are fully immersed in what is true for them. This becomes something that inspires and activates others into seeking what brings them joy in their lives. You make the most out of your human incarnation when you honour what is true for you; even if it is not what is true for another. There are many ways to live a human life, as well as many complex reasons one would choose to experience a human life to evolve on a soul level. Humans are often invited by their soul's higher consciousness to start making choices that are more supportive of their wellbeing- energetically, emotionally, mentally, and spiritually. It would serve you all well to trust those invitations from your higher consciousness and take the actions that feel most aligned towards better wellness. A humanity that is well emotionally, mentally, spiritually, and physically is a humanity that can hold loves vibration at its highest frequency, which serves one and all."

7. What is your guidance around our star families and how they influence us?

"Star families are your cosmic ancestry; your light source so to speak. The original light of creation from your inception. Having this knowledge is as important to you as your human ancestry.

Your Star families hold the energetic keys that help you access your soul gifts here on Earth. You are welcome to call on their support at any time and they will show up for you, to guide and support you as you navigate your life on Earth.

Our star families of origin influence our life path and the choices we make before we incarnate in each lifetime. They hold the original light codes, your original blueprint. You may have lived many versions of reality as a star being, or light being, as well as human being, yet there is one core star family of origin from which you are from. This first light from which you were created is what holds you throughout all space and time.

If you can imagine for a moment a golden thread and pouring from what you would call the heavens unto the Earth, into the centre of the Earth, rising upwards and moving downwards. Upon this thread is many beads of light, fractals of light, each with their own power source of light, that can extend, express and play in the source of all of creation. Gifting opportunities to experience the ascent and descent of creation. It is limitless what one can experience. Know too that all are held within the core thread, the one rod of light that anchors them fully to the original source, your original star family, as this is the thread of existence that holds memories of all you have learned, grown through, met, and lived through as a cosmic universal being.

Once you understand this, you will understand the importance of their role in your journey, no matter the assigned purpose, planet, or chosen form.

They guide you from a place of higher consciousness to stay aligned with our soul's mission, they hold us in the highest form of love no matter where our soul's journey takes us. They guide you on every incarnation and help you activate the gifts that live in you so that you can evolve as intended. As this question has been asked by a divine human, I would like to say that in your human life, your star family of origin helps you unlock your soul gifts that you have called forth before you took on your Earthly role in this lifetime. They will redirect you if you have wandered too far from the experience you chose to live for your highest evolution in this lifetime, ensuring you learn all you came to learn."

8. Will we come together and grow our own foods, cutting out the corruption within our food industries?

"This has begun in many small pockets of your world. Trust the seeds that have been planted. The corruption cannot stay given the changes that are coming for you all."

9. Will we become a world that helps each other?

"You live upon a world where many help each other daily. In every single moment there is more kindness than not, more compassion than not.

Every single time something shakes your planet to its core by the actions of a small few, more kindness is born. More of you show up to shower your communities in the love and support that is needed.

There is no lack of love, kindness or help on your planet. What there is a lack of is a trust that it is enough to shift the evolution towards the path of love it has always been destined to take."

10. How are our children influencing the collective?

"Today's children are shifting the parenting paradigm, the educational systems, the health systems, and governing bodies, and pushing humanity beyond the cultural normality of what has been lived for thousands of years. They are asking more of their lives, their parents, and those who are entrusted with their wellbeing. They are highly sensitive attuned souls. Some have entered the Earth for the first time; especially those born after 2006. They are New Earth children and are here to guide and anchor in light. Imagine the world is awash with diamond light, these diamonds are our children. They are opening and filling with light and then anchoring this light into the Earth's grid lines just by their presence. You best support them by ensuring they have environments that support their sensitivities and natural curiosity to explore this new world they find themselves in.

They are challenging to those of you who are strongly programmed into old ways of being. These children are here to challenge, here to soften, and here to remind us of what truly matters in this life. They will not work and grind their lifeforce energy away to feed a system of repression that seeks to undermine their soul gifts and missions.

They are here with purpose, and it will be known and felt by many as they continue to grow and evolve at this time. They know what they have signed up for entering the Earth's grid at this timeline of our evolution. Many are the first guardians of the New Earth and have within them knowledge to support humanity and the Earth through this momentous shift of the ages."

11. Why is it that every time we reincarnate, we must have our memories cleared and start over repeatedly?

"To arrive Earthside with every memory of your existence would be too much for one mind to hold. As you grow and evolve into claiming your soul's mission in your human form, your veil of forgetfulness begins to lift, and you begin to see and recall past lifetimes to support you in this lifetime. This is slowly brought to you over your lifetime so that you may anchor in the soul's gifts from past timelines to help you in this timeline. As Earth continues to evolve beyond the density of the last thousands of years, less and less of you will arrive Earthside with no memory of your origins and past life timelines. Some of you may already be witnessing this in today's children. If all of humanity remembered all at once the truth of your cosmic origins, and the truth of Earth's journey, it would create mass fear and the chaos that would arrive Earthside and would rupture more than Earth."

12. Will we reach a point of wholeness?

"You are never not whole. There is nothing to reach. All you need do is remember. Your very existence is whole unto one, universally so, cosmically so, humanly so."

13. How do we then evolve and move forward on Earth as a collective?

"You are currently evolving and moving forwards. You keep your hearts and minds open; you discern what is true for your soul's journey, you recognise the gifts in your humanity and experience in your life."

14. Will we always be striving towards wholeness?

"As long as you believe there is something wrong with you, you will always be striving. Humanity will find peace with itself when it recognises the gift of life on Earth."

15. Will we as a collective wake up to the sovereign power of our hearts and souls? Will we see a re-emergence of a re-awakened sacredness?

"Yes, this is well under way and there is continuous emergence of what it is to live in sacred alignment with all of life. There is much to yet walk through as a collective, and at times it may seem a never-ending spiral that moves backwards rather than forwards. Take heart, dear heart, that all is moving as it needs to."

Chapter Twenty Two
The Last Word

This path I walk chose me and I chose it in return

It is not a path you make time for; it is part of your very existence and is lived daily.

Chosen with devotion and daily intention as it asks that we let the heart lead.

It often asks that we have the courage to take space away from what is familiar. Particularly if what is familiar is causing us to doubt our capacity to choose what is right for us. It takes courage, stamina, and a willingness to keep diving inwards, so that we may find truths that resonate with our being.

It asks huge levels of trust when we are detangling the webs of confusion we have lived through and experienced in this life. It may require that we take space from those we love, even if only momentarily, so that we can see and know thyself truly outside of their influence. This is often the hardest part as it can begin to feel isolating and lonely at times. This path will make life uncomfortable and be a catalyst for change. Barriers to your heart's wisdom and truest expression will dissolve. So that you will rise fully, able to hold and contain all that you are with a steadfast love that knows and understands that many paths bring us back to love.

As you read these last words, place your hand upon your heart. Feel its beat, its purpose, your purpose. Know that you are loved that you deserve to take all the time and space in the world to become. When you learn to know yourself, you will begin to discern and choose your company wisely. You will crave safety, authenticity, honesty, respect, and finetune your bodily wisdom. You will discover that we are multi-dimensional. Collectively and individually, we are still very much splintered, divided, separated, far from mastery, and this is humbling for us all to know. We have so much to learn and much yet to grow through as a collective. Some of us are more physically and mentally strong, yet emotionally and spiritually weak. Others are spiritually and emotionally strong yet are physically weak and still mastering our health. We are all still fine-tuning our most precious instrument – our bodies. We anchor in what is sacred by recognising that we already are. We become through the embodiment of creation itself.

Imagine if you will those that are physically strong and focused on this aspect of our health and wellbeing are holding that thread and activating it for the whole. Those that are spiritually strong are holding that collective thread of collective creation strong for those yet to remember their divinity. We go on in and through this holy weave of creation until all threads of our divine remembrance open fully our sacred miraculous gift so we may know our inner power to co-create a new foundation that will hold us all in perfect alignment.

Whether we choose to believe, we are at a choice point for humanity and having a soul experience that is reminding us of our multi-dimensional existence. It is time to really sharpen our bodily temple and its wisdom. To strengthen the aspects of our humanity that have been weakened through the lens of distortions that exist on our planet. Pay attention to what you have been ignoring. Tap into the heart daily and ask on the inside- what have I not been aware of, listening to, or seeing clearly? Recognise your own body as the truth detector it is. Pay attention to what feels true and what does not. Sharpen your perception and ask if what is being brought to you is truth. Open the mind to the possibilities. Can you see that we are in fact miracles created with sacred intention for a divine purpose?

Gift yourself a moment daily and fill up with white light. Place your hands in front of you. Imagine a diamond has been placed within it. Imagine it opening and filling with white light. Place this diamond upon your crown or anywhere in your body that you feel called to. Imagine the diamond within you now opening and the white light moving throughout your body and entire energetic field- shielding and energising you all at once. Do this daily and repeat the following looking into your own eyes.

Soul whisper ~ Remember this

"I am a miracle created with loving sacred intention full of divine purpose."

There is a lot of noise, distractions, misinformation, and different versions of what is true. People afraid of our future, their future, people needing to be the only one who is right. Many paths, many truths. Find what yours is- trust it, claim it, walk it, live it, love it.

There is so much supporting our path home to love. A divine plan is actively alive. Everyone is looking for a big purpose, for their divine mission, and running around overcomplicating their lives with the mind, getting caught up in the distractions of the wounded ego.

Our mission is so simple: we are love, here to love and be loved in return. Love is what you are, love is what you have always been. Choose to love with all your being. Let love be your guide. Let that love lead the way. Let love speak through you. Let love create through you. Let love dance through you. Let love remember through you. Love shows up in so many ways in our lives. It can be the softest motherly blanket of love that creates a safe space to drop into and be for a moment. It can be the strict mother that pushes you forward, past your comfort zones, to stretch your being so you can hold more of the love that you are. It can give and it will take, depending on what is most necessary for your growth.

I leave you with this…

What is love asking of you- today, tomorrow and in this life?

In love devotion and gratitude always,

Your Soul Whisperer

Genevieve xxx

Destined to write

*Dedicated to those
of us still hurting*

Sacred Resources

The Soul Whispering Collective

1 to 1 mentorship

Connect with me here:

Genevieve Mc Guinness | Facebook www.genevievemcgee.com

Connect with Frankey here: www.ourpyschicart.com

IET: https://www.learniet.com

Testimonials

"Genevieve has been incredibly inspiring to many, many women who walk this path of remembrance with her. When you walk with this woman you have no choice but to bring your own gaze to your heart centre and seek there in the beauty that you behold." Majella

"Genevieve is a connector of women who connects us back to the parts we didn't even realise were missing, helping us answer questions we didn't even know needed asked." Stacey

"This woman continues to remember the ancient mysteries whispered and held within the hearts, wombs and bones of women. In remembering, she helps other women to do the same. This ancient remembrance is key to birthing our new Earth." Siobhan

"Soul Whisperer" gifted to her by the women she works with … let your soul be held in the ultimate safety, compassion and love." Joanie

Book list for further inspiration Book list for further reading:

Sacred Sexual Union by Anaiya Sophia

Fierce Feminine Rising by Anaiya Sophia

Witch by Lisa Lister

Code Red by Lisa Lister

Wild Power by Alexandra Pope & Sjanie Hugo Wurlitzer

Return of the Divine Sophia by Tricia McCannon Rise Sister Rise
by Rebecca Campbell

Anna, Grandmother of Jesus by Claire Heartsong

How To Do the Work by Dr. Nicole Lepera

Attached by Dr. Amir Levine and Rachel S.F Heller

Women Who Run with the Wolves by Clarrisa Pinkola Estes The
Magdalene Manuscript by Tom Kenyon & Judi Sion

Womb Awakening by Azra Bertrand M.D & Seren Bertrand
Disclaimer:

I, Genevieve Mc Guinness, am not a trained psychologist, counsellor, or medical professional. The information contained within this book is through my own personal perspective and experiences.

I trust you, the readers of this book, will know your own personal limits and have an awareness of when to seek out professional support along your own path of remembrance.

If you are unsure about any of the suggested practices in this book, please do consult with your own doctor or medical professional before you commit to it.

Thank you

Genevieve

May you always
know how sacred, holy
and loved you are.
Your Soul Whisperer